My Heart Cries Abba

DESTINY IMAGE BOOKS BY HANK KUNNEMAN

*Barrier Breakers: Ignite Your Faith, Stir Your Spirit,
Destroy the Works of the Devil Surrounding Your Life*

*Spiritual A.D.D.: Overcoming Spiritual Attention
Deficit Disorder*

*The Prayer from the Crypt: Keys to Reaching the Souls
of Your Loved Ones and Others*

My Heart
Cries
Abba

Discovering Your Heavenly Father
in a more Personal Way

Hank Kunneman

DESTINY IMAGE® PUBLISHERS, INC.
P.O. Box 310, Shippensburg, PA 17257-0310
"Promoting Inspired Lives."

This book and all other Destiny Image, Revival Press, MercyPlace, Fresh Bread, Destiny Image Fiction, and Treasure House books are available at Christian bookstores and distributors worldwide.

For more information on foreign distributors, call 717-532-3040. Reach us on the Internet: www.destinyimage.com.

ISBN 13 TP: 978-0-7684-0355-8
ISBN 13 Ebook: 978-0-7684-8485-4

For Worldwide Distribution, Printed in the U.S.A.
3 4 5 6 7 8 / 17 16 15 14

Contents

Chapter One

My Testimony

"Deny this Jesus or get out!" These were the words that I couldn't believe were coming out of my father's mouth. I had just given my life to the Lord and just graduated from high school. My salvation was one that I was deeply committed to and radical about, yet my zeal for the Lord was greater than my knowledge about how to reach my parents with the gospel.

My constant, bold approach to making sure my dad and mom were going to Heaven was more than my father would accept. He'd had enough and was now demanding that I make a choice between my newfound Christian walk and living in his home. I responded in opposition to his demands, as we were both yelling at each other, face to face, with a heated exchange of words. "I won't deny the Lord," I said. This made my dad even angrier that I wouldn't adjust, and he was now convinced that I was in a cult.

I had made him very angry especially with my bold declaration that I was being healed by the Lord. I had been dealing with a serious acne breakout for a few of my latter high school years, until something dramatic happened shortly after my graduation. I attended a church service where the pastor called out a word from the Lord that somebody was being healed of extreme acne. Being a new Christian, I thought this was ridiculous as I didn't know much about God's miraculous power at that time. I thought the minister was just saying that because, after all, I was in the second row. How could he miss me? Yet much to my surprise, within a very short time I started noticing what looked like someone had taken their hands to my acned cheeks leaving what had the appearance of fingerprints. There were different sized circles of clear skin appearing on both sides of my face as if someone had touched my face with their fingers.

This was more than my dad could handle and further fueled the heated exchange we were having at the top of the stairs. He stated it would be a cold day in hell before he would believe in miracles or my "born again" experience. The argument got so intense that the next thing I knew I was tumbling down the steps and landed at the bottom looking up at my dad, who was raging with anger.

How could this be happening? All I wanted was for my dad to accept Jesus, tell me that he loved me, and believe my story. With tears streaming down my face, I picked myself up, not fully realizing what had just happened, and walked to my room in my parent's basement. I sat on the edge of my bed, took a deep breath and began packing, even though I had nowhere to go and no money to speak of. I grabbed my clothes, a few items, and a sleeping bag. I headed out to my car to drive anywhere—anywhere away from the place where I just had the heated exchange with my dad. I will never forget the empty feeling and the surreal moment as I backed out of my parents' driveway, not sure what to do.

What Now?

I drove around the city thinking of different options as it was going to be dark soon. I began to reflect upon my life and this God to whom I had just committed my life. "Well, God, I guess I am Your problem now." I started to cry; and to make matters worse, I was listening to a very sad Christian song playing on my car stereo. My heart was racing and my hands were sweating on the steering wheel as I was thinking about what had just happened.

I pulled up to a pay phone (as this was many years before cell phones) and took a phone number out of my wallet. The number was from a young college-age man who I didn't really know very well, but had met at a church youth group I had visited two weeks prior. He had given me his number and told me, "If you ever need anything, give me a call." Staring at the number and hesitant to call this stranger, I almost put the number back in my wallet. What will it hurt? I thought, I don't have any place to stay. So I dialed the number with trepidation, trying to hold back my tears and act put-together. Thank God, he answered, I thought. "Hello, this is Hank, do you remember me? I met you at a youth group a couple weeks ago." I explained to him that I just had a fight with my dad and he kicked me out and I didn't have anywhere to go. "Yeah I remember you, come over and let's visit," he responded. I wasn't familiar with the address or part of town he was directing me to, but decided to drive toward his house.

I arrived at his address and parked on the street in front. It was dark so I couldn't really tell much about the house or neighborhood. I would soon discover that it was an old house that seemed to lean to the left when looking at it. The white paint was peeling off the wood siding and the front porch was black from exhaust due to the very busy traffic passing by on a main road. It was definitely not the best-kept house and was in an older part of town.

This old, rugged house was being rented by two young Christian military bachelors. I so appreciated that they were gracious enough to invite me in, hear me out, and even pray with me. As we visited for a moment they informed that their other roommate had just moved out and they had a room for me on the main level if I wanted to stay. "Sure," I said, swallowing hard after seeing a mouse scurry by and also seeing what would become my small room. It had a bed and a large ugly object in the corner. The object was a smelly, worn out, fold-out couch that wouldn't fit in the room unless tipped up on one end. The bottom was torn out of it with a few pieces of fabric remaining and some metal bars showing underneath. The bars would become my small "closet" to hang a few clothes on. Looking at the stained mattress, warped in the middle, and with no bedding, I wondered if I could afford to live here.

Struggling to sleep the first night in the sleeping bag that I had for bedding, I suddenly sat straight up awakened by something I hadn't heard before. This noise would become an all too frequent sound in my newfound "home." It was the sound of gunshots just outside my window. I would have to quickly adjust to the noise of a busy street, regular sounds of gunshots, and fights in the alley behind the house. This would be a bit much for me as I grew up in a fairly quiet suburban part of the city and never experienced these things before. I didn't realize that I had just agreed to move into what was a vastly different culture from what I was raised in.

It didn't take long for me to understand that I had a lot of growing up to do and needed God to help me more than ever. I didn't know how to cook much of anything and never applied myself to learn about how to budget or live life on my own. At least I had a job making a little money working at a gas station. If I didn't have enough cash for food after paying rent and utilities, I would often fast as it seemed easier to afford things this way.

Thanksgiving was quickly approaching and Christmas would be just around the corner after just a few months beyond the fight with my dad. My roommates were leaving for both holidays, and I wasn't going to let them know that I didn't have any family to spend the holidays with. What should I eat? I thought. It's Thanksgiving and people are supposed to eat turkey, right? Stabbing my fork into a piece of what looked like turkey in a TV dinner, I began to eat my first Thanksgiving dinner alone, staring out the window and shocked at the almost nonexistent traffic on a normally busy street in front of the house. I started to tear up because I was alone and revisiting my life growing up and what got me to this place. I quickly shook it off and thought to myself, Suck it up, Hank, there are plenty of people who don't have anything or anywhere to go on Thanksgiving.

Our Heavenly Father

Soon after it was the Christmas season and the first of which I would spend by myself, as this would become the norm for a few years. I would celebrate holidays alone, without any contact with my parents or family, and my roommates would leave town, going back to their families.

It was Christmas Eve and very cold due to poor insulation in the old house I was now living in. I could not only hear the wind, but even felt it blowing through the windows! Regardless, I decided to get into the Christmas spirit. Not being much of a decorator as I was barely out of high school, I purchased a small box of Christmas lights to hang in my bedroom. I decided I would read the Christmas story and sing a few songs to the Lord. What I didn't realize was that this time with the Lord would begin a journey toward God becoming more than just a belief system, more than just a casual acquaintance—He would become my heavenly Father. My heart would come to know God as Abba.

As I prayed and worshipped the Lord, not just that night, but many nights leading up to it, I thought about that horrible confrontation with my dad. I felt like what happened to me wasn't fair, but then again often life isn't fair. I still replayed the events in my mind and even reflected on my childhood and how I was just about a year old when my biological father had left my mother. They were married for a very short time before he left my mom with both my older sister and me.

I never knew or met my biological father, and he is no longer alive. However, recently after many years, I now have met some of his family and relatives. I had never known or met my biological father's side before he died and it wasn't until much later in my adult life. I must say it is still amazing to see some of my personality traits and features in people I had never met and their certain resemblance to me.

When I was around the age of two, my mom remarried, and the man became the only earthly father I would ever know. He became my stepdad and adopted me as his own. I never called him by his first name out of respect, or ever let anyone know that he was my stepdad, since I shared his last name. It hasn't been but recently that I have shared my story.

My relationship with my earthly father is the reason that my heart can cry out to God and call Him "Abba Father." "Abba," you say? Yes, and we will discuss throughout this book why calling God "Abba" is so important. Abba is a more intimate word for addressing God as our heavenly Father. I can call Him this because I truly understand the spirit of adoption. This is important because we can often relate our relationship with our heavenly Father to that of our earthly father. We live in a society today of broken homes, broken hearts, abuse of all kinds, abandonment, abortion, and a countless number of people who grew up without a father. Often, even if people did have a father when growing up, for many, there were few or no words of affirmation, and seldom if ever did they hear the words, "I love you." Some live with the memory of being entirely rejected by their earthly dad. I am sharing the story of my dad to help people—you—better understand that you are not alone, you are not abandoned or without hope.

Or perhaps your childhood was just the opposite and you grew up with a positive experience with your dad. My wife, Brenda, had a loving and God-fearing father. We cannot negate learning from those who grew up with this kind of love and stable life skills from early childhood. Brenda has exemplified godly love in more ways than I can describe; and because of our close-knit relationship, we have built a very stable Christian home.

That said, because our earthly experiences with our parents can vary so greatly, we all have to separate our personal experience from our revelation of the heavenly Father to some degree. This is because no earthly father can fully emulate who God is. So regardless of your story, God wants you to experience His Fatherly love in a divine and supernatural way that is unique to you.

For me, my earthly experience included my now step-dad who was a retired military airman. He was determined, extremely dedicated, hardworking, and a no-nonsense type of man. He took nothing off of anyone and always stood his ground, especially in what he believed was right. He was very opinionated about his beliefs, set and unwavering in them. He was not a churchgoer and believed religion was something of a private matter. He felt he had his own private "Christian beliefs" and mine were too extreme compared to his. He was, however, a man of extreme integrity and responsibility, which was the strength of his character. He always treated people fairly, honoring his word, and never set out to defraud anyone. Yet, he was like a lot of fathers today, who themselves grew up without the best example of what heartfelt love is in a home. For this very reason many dads don't know how to express love to their children.

My dad never abused me and tried to express love in his own limited way. At the same time, I never actually heard him say that he loved me while I was growing up. His way of love was to provide for his children, teach them the value of hard work and discipline, and to provide a roof over their heads. In his mind, that was all that was needed. Sure, he was a hard disciplinarian and stubborn in his beliefs, which is what led to our heated discussion and me getting kicked out of the house. It was what he considered demonstrating love the best way he knew.

Growing up for me was not always easy and wasn't without many feelings of rejection at times. Also contributing to this feeling was living in a home that was often divided because my adopted grandparents would sometimes make things difficult by dividing up the grandkids. My stepdad had four children of his own from a previous marriage and my mom had two, my sister and me from our biological father. After my mom and stepdad married, they had a daughter together—by terms, my "half-sister." My adoptive grandparents would spend extra time explaining to my sister and me that we were different, that we weren't their blood, and that our youngest sister, born to my mom and stepdad, was only half-blood. They would tell me that I would never be a real Kunneman, as this was impossible. They would let me know that I was not one of their favorites, often giving more expensive presents or additional presents to their blood grandkids over my sister and me. Sure this was hurtful, but being a child, I understood no other way than to see them as my own grandparents. I really believe God protected me and my heart through those times of my upbringing.

I know this protection from the Lord was partly due to a spiritual experience I once had when I was five years old when living on the island of Guam where my dad was stationed during his term in the military. This is when I believe that Abba God came to me in childlike terms, as His voice seemed to come from above one day as I leaned against my parents' car. He spoke inside my heart, in words that I would understand at a very young age, affirming His care, His affirmation, love, and plan for my life by simply "telling" me to always do what was right. After that experience, I always lived with the determination to do what is right.

After retiring from the military, my dad opened his own service station, and I worked for him pumping gasoline and doing light mechanical duties through my preteen and teenage years. We had a good working relationship, and that is what mostly defined our father and son times together. My dad was not one to compliment me on a job well done, as his method of teaching was you better get it the first time and you better do it right. I learned that no news or compliments meant I was doing well. My dad's patience would often be tested while working for him at the service station, as I struggled with fine "motor skills," literally with no pun intended.

Those times working with my dad were not to be taken for granted because not many get to spend that kind of time with their parents on a day-to-day basis, even if it is business related. My dad often mentioned later in life that those years when we worked together were very memorable for him. I would continue to work at my dad's service station even after he sold it and retired. It became the source of my small income after the confrontation with him that got me kicked out of the house. This is why it was very hurtful and confusing for me to have such a strained relationship after spending time working with my dad almost every day. After that confrontation, I didn't have much interaction with my parents for several years.

They softened a little when I married Brenda a few years later in 1989. She and I grew up together in the Lord and in ministry for several years, until we eventually launched a church together in 1997. Although my dad softened toward me on a surface level, he still remained set in his beliefs and would not have much to do with my ministry or the church I pastored. The times we did spend together were often awkward and lacked any father-son bond. It continued like that until something happened after two decades of being asked to leave his home.

Healing

I remember the call from my mom as if it was yesterday. She was very upset as she was telling me that my dad had just been diagnosed with stage four lung cancer. I prayed with my mom and tried to reach out to my dad, who seemed to be a little more open than he used to be about healing and having me pray for him. This was a surprise because previously he had been so resistant to any talk of miracles.

What I didn't know was that my dad had been watching my live-stream church services on Sundays for quite a few months and had been enjoying it. I could hardly believe the news of this! So I thought I would get even bolder and ask him if I could have a friend of mine pray for him. The friend was Richard Roberts, the son of Oral Roberts, who has a very strong healing ministry, like his father, with staggering numbers of documented people who have been healed from cancer. I will never forget calling my dad to set up a time for Richard to call him—and not sure of the response I would receive. To my surprise again, he agreed.

Amazing things began to happen in my dad's health after Richard prayed for him, and in that process Richard also had an opportunity to lead my dad to the Lord! What was even more incredible was the fact that the doctors couldn't believe my dad's continually improving condition after he was prayed for. They were witnessing a huge touch from God as the cancer was shrinking, and with their own admission saying they couldn't believe or explain it. Yet, something else was happening. My dad was softening, changing, and becoming tender due to his prayer of salvation and seeing God healing him.

This is why we must never give up on our loved ones and must keep praying for them. I watched a divine change happen in my dad's life. He was beginning to express tender love. In fact he started saying for the first time the words, "I love you."

I'll never forget the day my dad called and said he wanted to talk to me about some things. It made me nervous and feel a bit uneasy. I wasn't sure why he wanted to meet with me as this was not his way and certainly out of character. I picked him up for lunch and started to drive with my hands sweating on the steering wheel. This is odd, I thought. The last time my hands were sweaty while trying to drive was once in a terrible snow storm and the other when I was driving around not knowing where I was going to live after the argument with my dad that got me kicked out his house. Yet, now I was in the car with my dad and my hands were sweaty again. This time though, instead of being at odds with each other we were starting to have the relationship that we both wanted. And now my dad wasn't resistant to the gospel because he had given his life to Jesus! I realized, after many years, that when my dad and I had the confrontation at the top of the stairs that he wasn't so much saying "deny Jesus" as much as he was associating my radical conversion to being in a cult.

We drove to lunch and visited for most of the afternoon, spending it looking at the place where he grew up. I know he could tell I was a bit nervous and spoke up saying something that shocked me. He said, "Hank, I am not afraid to die. I am at peace with myself and at peace with God. Tell me a little bit about Heaven." His words surprised me. He also mentioned how he wished he would have done some things differently in the way he raised me, and also for allowing his parents to create tension in the family over who was or wasn't a "real" Kunneman. He continued to say how he was remorseful for kicking me out of the house and that he always thought of me as His own and appreciated that I treated him the same way.

As we drove up his driveway, we talked some more about Heaven and how some of his beliefs had changed. He said, "At one time, I didn't believe the way I do now. I never believed in miracles, but I do now...especially with what I have seen happen in my own life." It was awesome to see how much the Lord was working in him.

"I want to give you something before you leave," he said. So I walked into his house as he handed me a bright yellow unopened package that contained an old tow rope. "Here, this is yours," he said. "I thought you might need this for one of your cars." I gladly accepted it, and to this day it has become special to me in that I now realize it symbolizes my upbringing and his conversion to Jesus. You see, it was he who had towed me along in life, being a provider and showing me how to do things the right way in life, even if there wasn't a verbal word of love or obvious expression of it. Nonetheless, he was still towing me, pulling me in a direction that was best for me, and helping me accomplish things correctly in life. What was more impacting is that later in his life, I was towing him, pulling him into a life of salvation in Jesus Christ. It had become obvious that his heart was transformed to feel and express the love of Jesus.

Feeling God's Love

I don't know about you, but there is something so special when we feel God's love for the first time, certainly once we are saved. We feel His tender peace, comfort, and love. It was similar to how I felt when I heard my dad tell me he loved me, and seeing the love in his heart he was now expressing. It was the same kind of feeling when you give your heart to the Lord, which is greater than any word could express.

I am not bitter over how I was raised or angry about the confrontation I had with my dad all those years ago. How could I be? After all, he had changed, and I also changed. Then ultimately, through it all, my dad came to know Abba, Father, and committed his life to Jesus.

In 2013, my dad went home to be with the Lord. However, it's not goodbye but rather, "Dad, I will see you later!" He is experiencing God's love in a whole new way as he began to experience it and express it before he left this earth. In fact, one day not long after his death, I was throwing a stack of papers away. As I began tossing them into the trash, all but one piece made it into the garbage. As it fell to the ground, I picked it up and saw that it was a short handwritten note. Little did I know that it was a note that my dad had written to me. To think I almost threw it away. At the end of his note were the words I was longing to hear from him much of my life, and it was his last written note to me. He signed it, "Take care, LOVE YOU, Dad!"

It is touching to me that not only did my dad get to experience God's love here on earth but now he is in Heaven and gets to see Him face to face. This is why we never should quit believing for our relatives. Most of all, no matter how we have been raised or what our relationship was with our earthly fathers, even if it never turned out positively, we can experience Abba's love that can fulfill what our earthly father did not. Whether it was a divine turnaround with our earthly dad or a divine touch from our heavenly Father, each of us can have an experience that causes our heart to cry, "Abba Father."

Discovering "Abba Father"

Being able to cry, "Abba Father" was what I had to rely on as I journeyed into my young adult life and grew older. I discovered that I am adopted into the heavenly Father's love and His family. It's the reason I wrote this book and I wanted to open it with my story, so I can help others know Abba God more intimately—no matter how they were raised. I share this story simply to celebrate who my dad became in his later years and where he is today.

I want you to know that you too can experience this love and revelation, even receiving healing from a broken heart, abandonment, or pain that perhaps came through your experience with your earthly father.

I pray that the chapters in this book will touch you deeply as Abba is revealed. My prayer is that you will feel His presence and see how God took me on a journey about God's Fatherly love. He took me from Genesis to Revelation revealing Abba to me—and is waiting to reveal Himself to you in a more intimate and personal way. You will find that God wants to be more than just Almighty God in your life—He wants to be your heavenly Dad who will never leave you or forsake you!

It's time for your heart to begin to cry, "Abba!"

Are you ready?

Turn the page and discover Him!

Chapter Two

God Becomes a Dad

*And [Jesus] said, Abba, Father, all things
are possible unto Thee; take away this cup
from Me: nevertheless not what I will, but
what Thou wilt* (Mark 14:36).

He fell to the ground, feeling the weight of the whole world upon His shoulders. He opened His mouth to utter a prayer as He fought through the agony of His own soul. His sweat, now turning to blood, began flowing from His brow and down His face, landing upon the ground on which He lay to pray. He opened His mouth to reveal His heart and to cry out to someone who possessed the greatest love He had ever known. It had now come to this moment. The one He was born for and would die for. Just whom would He cry out for and in whom would He put His trust?

Heaven stood watching to see what He would do and hell looked intensely at the suffering of God's Son. The very One sent from Heaven. They were listening to what would come from His lips. "Abba, Father!" Jesus cried from deep within.

Whom was He crying out to and why? What did this mean? The sound of "Abba" rang out from the earth and reached the very throne of Heaven as Jesus, the Son of God, prayed in agony. He was now facing His greatest time of need in His earthly life. His heart was crying for Abba, His Father. Prior to that time, knowing that He would be facing that moment, He had invited a few of His followers to pray with Him, only to find them sleeping instead! Was there no one He could count on but the One who promised not to leave Him alone and who was committed to stay by His side?

Think for a moment of what security, what love, and what reassurance He must have felt in calling out to the One He referred to as Abba. Imagine all the things Jesus could have said at that moment of suffering, and He chose to say, "Abba." After all, this is what He taught His disciples to do as well—when you pray say, "Father" (see Luke 11:2). We must understand, that day in the Garden of Gethsemane He wasn't just saying "Father" in a formal sense alone. Rather by His use of this name, Jesus was reaching out to a deeper personal God whom He had come to know as His heavenly Daddy. Is this right? A grown man, a carpenter not known for being weak, is now using such a term in His native Aramaic language. If this word was to be reserved for small toddler-age children addressing their earthly fathers as daddy, why would He choose this word in addressing His Father? What does it mean and why would Jesus call His heavenly Father "Abba"?

Jesus Revealed Abba

In order to answer these questions and comprehend the deep love Jesus had toward the One He referred to as Abba, we need to understand who He is and why Jesus used this word.

Perhaps the reason Jesus addressed His heavenly Father in this manner was because of the long relationship He had with Him before the foundations of the earth were made. Better yet, maybe it was because He had come to know His heavenly Father even more intimately due to living upon this earth and being fully dependent upon Him as a human under the power of the Spirit. This may be in part due to growing up, at some point, without His earthly father, Joseph, whom we don't hear much about after we see Jesus debating in the temple at the age of 12. However, what we can conclude is that in the time of the Lord's greatest need, He called out to Abba and also spent His entire ministry revealing Him as an intimate Father, loving to be in relationship with His children.

Jesus prayed to Him, *"I have revealed You to those whom You gave Me out of the world"* (John 17:6 NIV). He didn't just do this for His benefit only, but also for you and me. He wants us to experience this same awesome, personal, intimate relationship with our heavenly Father as He did. After all, this was the reason He was sent to the earth—to reveal Abba Father and reconcile us back to Him.

As we reflect on the name *Abba*, it is not surprising that perhaps some of us didn't grow up with a father, or maybe others did but it wasn't a good experience. Then there are others who grew up with an earthly father and it was a positive experience. Whatever the scenario faced, the encouraging thing is that we all have access to God who supersedes any earthly examples of a father. Jesus came to reveal Him so we could have the joy, peace, and fulfillment of being loved by a heavenly Father, a heavenly Daddy called Abba!

You might be thinking that calling God your heavenly Daddy or Papa seems strange or it's just hard to make the correlation in your personal life. This is often due to the earthly example you had as a father or have seen in others, so it becomes uncomfortable and bit awkward to see God as a loving Father.

But the reason Jesus called God Abba, was to reveal to us that it is in fact okay to refer to Him as such! This is so we can have the same kind of awesome relationship with Him just like Jesus had. Remember, God wants to reveal Himself as Abba, and this is why He sent Jesus to show the whole world, from generation to generation, including you and me, this amazing attribute! He longs for us to approach Him as a loving Father, not a harsh taskmaster.

In fact, we need to take a closer look at Abba and its definition because it will only strengthen our relationship with Him and take away any reservations or feelings of inadequacy when addressing Him as such. Once we understand who He is, our hearts will most certainly cry out, "Abba, Father!"

Who Is Abba?

The definition of Abba can be compared in our English language to the word daddy or papa. A further examination of the word will find that it is mentioned specifically three other times in the New Testament. It is part of the Aramaic dialect that was used during the life of Jesus by the Jews, describing a more personal, intimate way of addressing God as our Father.

The word *Abba* is translated in the *Strong's Concordance* as "ab" (awb), which is a more formal definition of God rather than Abba. *Abba* is an Aramaic word, meaning "Daddy" or "dear Father"; a term of endearment, not as formal as the word "ab." The word *Abba* means "Father," and is used by a beloved child in an affectionate, dependent relationship with their father; "daddy," "papa."

In fact, what is even more exciting in the study of this word is found in an article written by David Alsobrook, called "Why Did Jesus Call God 'Daddy'?" He writes:

> What would you think of a grown man who walked around saying, "My daddy says this…my daddy says that…I only do what I see daddy doing, and I only speak what I hear daddy saying"? This is precisely the way our Savior spoke around everyone, including the respected religious leaders of His day. None of His hearers had uttered the word "daddy" since they were tots. Jesus called God "Daddy" more than 170 times in the Gospels![1]

The word for *daddy* was the Aramaic and Hebrew word *abba*. There was another word young children past the toddler stage called their paternal parent as well: *abinu*. In the more than 170 places in the Gospels where Jesus refers to God in the parental role, He consistently calls Him "Abba" each time. Not once did the Son of God refer to His Begetter as "Abinu"! This is amazing when you stop and consider it: He used the toddler's word for His Father. All the school-aged children in Israel called their fathers "abinu," never "abba."[2]

It is amazing to see just how much the Lord wants to be more than just a great all-powerful God. He wants to be our heavenly Daddy! This truth can be seen in a closer examination of the word *Abba*. The first part, *ab*, is a standard word which means "Father." The second word is *ba*, which is used to make this word a form of addressing someone. For example, if a person is referring to someone's father, they would most likely use the word *Ab*, meaning father. Yet, if you were to use the word Abba, putting the two words together, it then becomes a more intimate, personal, and relational way of speaking about your dad, papa, or father. So when you address God as Abba, you are saying by the translation of this word, "My dearest Father, Papa, and Daddy!" Those are intimate terms.

It is also interesting to note that when the word Abba appears in the New Testament combined with the word Father, it is to imply something deep about God's heart and nature. For example, Paul wrote, *"For ye have not received the spirit of bondage again to fear; but ye have received the Spirit of adoption, whereby we cry, Abba, Father"* (Rom. 8:15).

When Abba and Father are connected together, it helps to further reveal God's love to all races and mankind. The word *Abba* is Aramaic, the language the Jews used during the time of Jesus, while the word *Father* is translated in the Greek to reach the Gentiles. The Lord is trying to reveal to us that He is the heavenly Father to both the Jews and the Gentiles and all the ethnos of mankind! That means that no matter what race or color we are, we are dearly loved and accepted by our heavenly Father as one of His own. He is not a respecter of persons, but a loving heavenly Daddy who wants to reveal Himself to us and take great care of us in the process.

It is such an awesome privilege that we can refer to God as our heavenly Dad by personally and intimately calling Him Abba, our heavenly Papa and Daddy. This brings such incredible love and a sense of belonging when we know that Jesus was revealing Abba to us throughout His time on the earth. It was not just as a Father figure, but an intimate heavenly Father or Daddy!

We can even see before the foundation of the world and the creation of all things that something was stirring deep inside the very heart and being of God almighty. It was something so dear that nothing in creation could match its worth, its value, or even be worth dying for. Inside the inner core of God's heart were the thoughts of you and me, which transcended into a deep longing to be a heavenly Daddy to all mankind.

Before All Things:
Father or Daddy?

It is important to understand that even though God wanted to be a heavenly Daddy to us, the very handiwork of His created brilliance, something would have to be accounted for before that could happen. What would that be? It is something every earthly father has the responsibility of asking, the same question God would have to ask Himself: Does Creator mean Daddy? What is the difference between Him being our Father, who created us, and our Abba?

In order to answer that question and get a glimpse of what was going on in the heart of God, we need to examine what the difference is between someone being a father or a daddy. First and foremost, just because a man can produce a child through his seed doesn't mean he is a daddy. It is the same way with God; just because He could create the first man, Adam, out of the dust of the earth as a loving Creator, does *not* qualify Him to be considered a heavenly Daddy. Isaiah said, *"Yet, O Lord, You are our Father. We are the clay, You are the potter; we are all the work of Your hand"* (Isa. 64:8 NIV).

When understanding the difference between a father and a daddy, we can see that there are generally three types of father figures prevalent today. First, there are biological fathers who provide the DNA to conceive a child through sexual relations but do not become a part of the child-rearing process. This is because the fathering role was only limited to producing offspring but did not uphold their commitment to parenting the child they produced. So the end result is that the child grows up without a father in their life or home.

Secondly, there are the provider and protector fathers who provide food, clothing, and a roof over the child's head throughout his or her life. The things this type of father provides often come without saying, "I love you," or heart-to-heart connections with the child. The father doesn't give much quality time, attention, affection, affirmation, or involvement in the child's life. This is due in large part to the focus being more about the role of a father that provides and protects than the heart of a father connecting with the child. Sometimes this can be a result of how the father of the child was raised himself; maybe they didn't experience a father saying to them, "I love you," on a consistent basis. Their expression of love was more implied by their actions to provide for their children than in saying it with words—it was not as much expressed by communicating and demonstrating their love on a regular basis that went beyond provision.

Lastly, there are those who represent biblical fathers that are like Abba Father in Heaven, where they love, affirm, and connect heart to heart and not just in a material provider way. They give their children their love, heart, time, attention, and dedication. The more the father expresses these different kinds of characteristics, the more secure, stable, affirmed, and loved the child feels. These are the attributes of what Abba represents.

This is why God had to look within His own heart and consider whether He would be a mere Creator or a personal Daddy in whom we could run to in our times of trouble. He would have to consider this question and even the scenario of foreknowing that man would sin and be separated from Him. This would have to be considered before He would ever create mankind. Would He only make man in His image but then disappear, forsake, and leave the children to a sin-ridden world? Would He be a heavenly Father who would protect and provide for His children, but without expressing love, affirmation, or affection? Or would He breathe His spiritual DNA into man, thus committing to provide and love by being deeply involved in His children's lives? In other words, would He allow Himself to become a heavenly Daddy and not just a Creator or Provider?

This is an important question to ask, after all, because God is our Father in the sense of being our Creator: He is the One who made us. This is why Moses asks the children of Israel before entering the Promised Land, *"Is this the way you repay the Lord, O foolish and unwise people? Is He not your Father, your Creator, who made you and formed you?"* (Deut. 32:6 NIV). God is our Father, the one who created us and formed us.

In other words, God is saying, "Yes, I am your Creator, I made you. Yet I am also your Father and will stick with you through every situation. I will never leave you or forsake you. I am your heavenly Daddy, and I care for you more than any angel, created being, or anything I have made, both in Heaven and on earth. I want to be involved in your life and I am committed to show you that throughout the entirety of your life." This is why He is more than our Creator; He is our heavenly Daddy too!

Made In God's Image

The decision by God to be more than just our Creator, to be our heavenly Father as well, would definitely become a decision worth dying for.

One of the ways in which we understand God's heart to be our Abba is to carefully look at the beginning days of creation. We see that our heavenly Father and Jesus, the Only begotten Son of God, were working together to make many things for a family He would create and become the Father of! It was Father and Son working together!

In the book of Proverbs, Jesus is spoken of as the personification of wisdom; but notice how He was alongside Abba at the creation:

> *When He gave to the sea His decree, that the waters should not pass His commandment: when He appointed*

the foundations of the earth: then I was by Him, as one brought up with Him: and I was daily His delight, rejoicing always before Him (Proverbs 8:29-30).

We can see from this Scripture the closeness that Jesus and His Father had even before there was time and as the world was being framed. This gives a beautiful picture of how Abba wants to work with us in our lives as well. Think for a moment about these days of creation, and how the Father and Son worked together! It can be compared to a father and son working together on a school project, creating a masterpiece.

It is truly incredible to see Abba and Jesus laboring together to create something that would reflect a deep, personal longing inside of them. This is revealed in those first few powerful words that would be spoken in regards to their most prized creation of all—mankind! It brings a new meaning and understanding to, *"Let Us make man in Our image"* (Gen. 1:26).

You might be wondering how that could be? Well, consider for moment what image Abba and Jesus were referring to. Not only was it speaking of man being created in the image of God as a being, but it also represented the image of a family. We can understand the great motive of love as we consider this statement: *"Let Us make man in Our image."* Again, it wasn't just the fact that we were created in His image to look, act, and be like God in our human form. But it was also the image of the family that God would create that would emulate and reflect the image of who Abba is and what He shared with His only begotten Son!

By making mankind, He would now extend and create sonship that would include all those born into the earth that would receive it. He would create man to be part of His family and He would be our heavenly Daddy. It is the image of Father and His children working together to be shared with every human being!

In other words, not only was it the Trinity speaking together as they said, *"Let* Us *make man in* Our *image,"* but it was also revealing Abba's desire for an extended family to include the Father, Son, Holy Spirit, and we, the church—all of us working together in the earth! It was a decision and announcement saying, "Let Us make man to be like Us, in Our image of Daddy and Son!" It would be Dad, Son, and His created children, loving each other, working together throughout all of time!

They were saying, "What We are together as Father, Son, and Spirit, We will give to the human race as well. We will be a family together! I, as God, will be their Father, and they will be My sons and daughters." It was to be just like the Father and Son working together in creation. They would now work with us, the human race, loving each other as a family, both in Heaven and on earth! The apostle Paul had this revelation and wrote it down for us: *"For this cause I bow my knees unto the Father of our Lord Jesus Christ, of whom the whole family in heaven and earth is named"* (Eph. 3:14-15).

When we commit our lives to Christ, we are part of one big spiritual family that encompasses both Heaven and earth when. I can imagine Abba speaking as part of the Trinity with such excitement as He began the process of creating a family on earth: "It will be in Our image. Let *Us* do it. We will make them in Our image, of Dad and Son, full of our Spirit! Let's go for it and make one big family!"

Abba's Questions

God knew the price of creating mankind in His image. In all of the previous five days of creation, God said "Let there be…" as He brought things forth out of what He created. However, this sixth day He wouldn't speak to the earth or heavens, but rather spoke to Himself, reproducing His image, starting a human race with His spiritual DNA: *"And God said, Let Us make man in Our image, after Our likeness..."* (Gen. 1:26).

Yet, again, this doesn't mean He was ready or qualified to be a spiritual Daddy. Again, creator doesn't mean daddy. Many men have procreated but then left the child to either die or become abandoned—they have failed to be daddies even though they were a child's father. But this would not be the case with God. He would not only create His sons and daughters, but stand by them, being their heavenly Daddy.

We know this by the first two questions recorded in Scripture that God asked of Adam and Eve. In both of these questions, they reveal the heart, character, attributes, and qualities of a true daddy. It shows that God truly would become Abba to the human race! In order for Him to make one big family and be the Father of the children He would create, He would have to be willing to take responsibility for us and bear the burden of caring for us. It is important for all of us to understand how much He loves us and is forever committed to us, if we will commit our lives to Him in return.

I learned this as I was driving in a very bad ice storm some time ago. I live in Nebraska where the winter can become very snowy and icy. This means you have to slow down and drive carefully because the roads can become extremely dangerous and slippery. I was gripping the wheel of my car and driving slowly as the conditions were worsening. I called out to God and said, "Lord, I need Your help and I ask You to watch over me as I drive in this storm."

I heard the Lord respond to me, "Hank, why wouldn't I take care of you and watch over you. After all, I am your Abba." It was at that moment I realized, knowing previously the definition of the word *Abba*, that God wanted to reveal to me that He wasn't just almighty God, He wasn't just my formal heavenly Father whom I have come to revere and fear; but He is my heavenly Daddy watching over me, loving, and caring for my very well-being. The moment He revealed Himself as Abba settled it for me. It was that experience that started me searching to find out more about Him and to write this book to reveal Him even further.

In the same way, God would have to be committed if He was going to make mankind and become a heavenly Daddy to us. But just when did God become a heavenly Daddy? Was it at the moment we were conceived in His mind or was it when He spoke desiring to make us in His image? How about at the moment He breathed His first breath into Adam? In all of those moments it was stirring in Him, but it didn't really manifest until He came seeking sinful Adam and Eve as they were hiding from Him in the Garden. This is why the first two questions are so significant, because they reveal God as Abba!

As we stated before, God Himself had to decide what relationship He would have with this mankind He would create. Would He be just our Creator or our personal Abba? It has always been in the heart of God to be our loving, caring, providing, affirming, affectionate, and passionate heavenly Daddy. However, it wasn't enough to just be in His heart. It would have to be demonstrated, as we see in His pursuit of His fallen children in the Garden.

This is why we can conclude through Scripture that Jesus was not only revealing Abba, but the first recorded questions in the Bible show that God was committed to being our heavenly Father. We see that He wanted to be more than our Creator— He longed to be our personal heavenly Father!

Think for a moment of the day Adam and Eve sinned and became separated from God. They chose to hide from Him in their fear and shame. They made fig leaves to cover their nakedness and sin. I am sure there were questions running through their minds, "How will God react to this? How will

He respond?" We can learn a lot about God wanting to become our heavenly Father, our personal Abba, by what God asked after they sinned. You could say that this was the day God really stepped into parenting and revealed that He was Abba forever! God showed mankind that he became a Dad!

"Adam, where are you?" God asked, as He walked in the Garden in the cool of the day (see Gen. 3:9). Didn't God already know where he was and what had taken place? Of course the answer is yes since God is all-knowing. Yet it reveals something more important going on here. It reveals God as Abba, His heart and love for His creation. This question, being the first recorded question in Scripture and the first spoken by God that is mentioned, showed that God was intending to be more than just a Creator for humankind, but a Daddy! It revealed the relationship He desired with His creation!

This intention is revealed through the cry of God, who was concerned for the well-being of His children He had created. He wouldn't leave them or forsake them in their sin. He wouldn't kick them when they were down. He wouldn't discipline them out of unjust hatred or anger. He was calling out to reveal Himself as Abba to them as they hid from His presence.

Think for a moment about His question, "Adam, where are you?" This is about relationship more than location. It reveals that He wants to spend time with us in a Father-Son relationship. But the second question God asked reveals even more concerning Abba, and is a question of provision, protection, concern, and responsibility: *And He said, Who told thee that thou wast naked? Hast thou eaten of the tree, whereof I commanded thee that thou shouldest not eat?* " (Gen. 3:11).

"Who told you that you were naked?" God asked. This revealed His responsibility as their heavenly Papa or He wouldn't have asked or been concerned about it in the first place. We see here from this question that He was indeed showing responsibility, asking who had messed with His children. Of course God already knew, but He was showing Himself as Abba, our Protector, being concerned about our well-being. He was essentially asking, "Who took something from you?"

He even followed up with an additional question, asking if they ate of the tree He told them not to eat from. This shows that it was their responsibility as well as ours to honor Him as their heavenly Father. He was also showing that He was a heavenly Dad who will discipline us in love if needed. That is what makes a good parent. They love, provide, protect, train, instruct, and even discipline us when needed.

We can certainly learn from these questions, about who our heavenly Father is and also what our priorities should be in seeking and loving Him in return.

God was more concerned for the whereabouts of His children as He called out to them. This revealed His heart commitment in desiring relationship and fellowship with Adam and Eve above all else. He knew because of their sin that this relationship dynamic had changed. Yet, what it says to us is the importance of prioritizing with God, that relationship with Him is more important than the provision and benefits He provides for us, which can be seen in the second question He asked.

These things that Abba asked reveal such deep truths—we belong, we are cherished. First and foremost, these questions reveal that He is our Daddy. Then, secondly, we gain an understanding of His many benefits, including providing for and protecting us.

As we seek to know Him more intimately, let's never forget what grieved Abba about the children of Israel in the wilderness. They often had things backward, showing their ingratitude to Him instead of rejoicing in what He had given them. They tended to seek His hand or His benefits first without prioritizing relationship with Him and seeking Him as the most important objective in their lives. They desired what they could personally benefit and receive of Him before showing a desire to have a personal, intimate relationship with Him. The psalmist wrote about this difference with Moses and the children of Israel: *"He made known His ways unto Moses, His acts unto the children of Israel"* (Ps. 103:7).

This is what God wants from you, me, and every person born into this world—an intimate relationship with Him as our Abba. I pray that Abba is starting to be revealed to you even more as you are feeling His love toward you. Never forget those words that were upon His lips and how He showed His love toward His creation by asking, "Where are you?" This is the cry of love from a caring heavenly Father, saying, "I want to be your heavenly Daddy and pour My blessings upon your life. I am not just your Creator, but your heavenly Abba, your very Daddy."

Let's never forget that He is still calling out to us today, daily waiting by our bedside the moment we open our eyes to call out His name. Oh, what an Abba we have! Now if only the world could see Him, they would surely come to love Him. How could they not, once they understand God's heart of love and compassion for them?

If they only knew God is not just their Creator, or God almighty, but a true heavenly Father who wants to show them who He is. In order for this to happen, however, we have to understand what a true father example really is. This is why it is so vital to see that Abba Father was not just a God who would be a masterful Creator, but One who would become a heavenly Daddy to those He created. He was committed to His creation, to you and me, forever!

Characteristics of a True Dad

We come to know how much God is committed to us when we understand His character. Sometimes, however, this can become clouded, tainted, or our relationship with Him hindered by unfair misunderstandings of God because of the parental examples we have had in our lives. We see this today in the broken relationships between children and their fathers. Sadly, this has become a real problem and has led to much of the pain that people face as a result, including feeling hurt, let down, and abandoned by God. In addition, it has also led some to not fully understanding the awesome fatherly characteristics of Abba God.

One can only fully comprehend who He is when we first realize what a true father is by the example God shows us throughout Scripture. And once we see that, then we need to understand that bad and hurtful examples of earthly fathers are in no way a reflection of who God is. It helps to understand what a true father is according to the biblical example of Abba. Because when we do, it will help to heal any hurts, disappointments, or feelings that keep us from trusting God completely.

Let us consider some of the earthly traits of a father and see how they reveal Abba in a more intimate way. Even Jesus said that if we have seen Him, then we have seen His Father (see John 14:9). So, what are the roles of an earthly daddy or father? We would have to start with love because everything starts and should be rooted in love when speaking of earthly fathers. This is expressed by words, actions, care, and by taking time to make their children a priority in their lives.

Secondly, the role of earthly fathers is seen in the need to understand the importance of regular dialogue with their children that goes beyond lecturing or instructing them. It requires fathers taking time to understand and listen to their children's needs, desires, and wants. Their role, thirdly, is also to be available and accessible to their children, showing that they are a priority and focus. Fathers are never to become so busy that they exclude their children in their schedules, but should make them a part of their daily lives and routines.

Fourthly, fathers are to protect and provide for their children, letting them always feel safe in their arms and presence. This will help them not be afraid to be around us, but rather receive a peace that Dad has their back. Their responsibility is to work hard, laboring to provide the very best they can for their children.

And lastly, fathers lead by example as they live out what is right and godly. This will encourage children to respect their fathers and take in a sense of values, love for God, and a knowing of right and wrong.

In all of these earthly traits and responsibilities, we can certainly see the qualities of Abba as our heavenly Dad. He, of course, is the perfect image of a true father and what the roles of earthly fathers should be modeled after. He will certainly love us, wanting to take time to have meaningful dialogue with us throughout the day, and not just restricting Himself to our daily devotions. He wants to connect with us and laugh with us, showing His character and attributes on a daily basis. He is interested in spending time with us, providing for us in every area of our lives, as well as protecting us in every situation we encounter. He is always available and deeply cherishes our moments with Him and longs for our attention to Him. He is also a great teacher and comforter who desires to help us and instruct us in our daily decisions, helping us through life. He is truly our heavenly Abba!

He also loves to affirm us and show us that He is pleased with us. He is not afraid to express His pleasure in us. He isn't like some earthly fathers who seldom affirm their children or only show their approval by not saying anything at all. In other words, no news or words of approval means we are doing things okay.

This isn't Abba's, our heavenly Daddy's, ways. He is not prideful, ashamed, timid, or stingy in affirming us or showing His approval. He revealed this when it came to Jesus, His Son. Think for a moment of the affirming words, the excitement over Jesus's ministry in the earth. We see examples of Abba speaking out of Heaven for all to hear of His approval and affirmation. He was saying as a proud heavenly Father, "God job, Son; I approve of You."

This is shown at the beginning of Jesus's ministry—"And lo a voice from heaven, saying, This is My beloved Son, in whom I am well pleased" (Matt. 3:17)—as well as during His ministry—"While He yet spake, behold, a bright cloud over-shadowed them: and behold a voice out of the cloud, which said, This is My beloved Son, in whom I am well pleased; hear ye Him" (Matt. 17:5).

Everybody needs affirmation, especially from their father. This is why Jesus received affirmation from His Father at the start of His ministry and also throughout His time on earth. He needed it, especially considering those that were constantly criticizing and accusing Jesus wrongly. Abba knew this and wanted His Son to be validated, and He wanted everyone to know it. He was one proud Father, saying, "Hey world, this is My Son: listen to Him!"

God so wants to affirm us and let us know that we are accepted in the Beloved (Abba)! This is why Paul wrote in Ephesians: *"To the praise of the glory of His grace, wherein He hath made us accepted in the Beloved"* (Eph. 1:6).

If you haven't had much affirmation from your earthly father, rest assured that your heavenly Father affirms you. In fact, He rejoices over you with singing! Zephaniah said of God, *"The Lord thy God in the midst of thee is mighty; He will save, He will rejoice over thee with joy; He will rest in His love, He will joy over thee with singing"* (Zeph. 3:17). The songs He is singing are songs of affirmation and love to you.

This should give us a great sense of affirmation from Abba. We are special. We are loved and accepted by Him. And He wants the whole world and all things created, both invisible and visible, to know that we are His child. He affirms you and accepts you!

Traits of Our Abba Father

Not only does He affirm us as His children, but His love is revealed toward us as we understand what love is and how it is defined.

Throughout history mankind has sought to know what true love is. They have mistaken it for what the world has defined it to be, and, even after they have tasted of what it has to offer by the way of love, they still walk away empty. In the midst of their pain, heartache, and disappointments, they still never come to an understanding of what true love is, so they continue to live in loneliness, failed relationship after failed relationship. After several failed attempts, they eventually give up, never fully understanding what true love is. Some feel as though they cannot go on another day without experiencing this love. They question God and they question themselves, eventually closing themselves off to any kind of love whatsoever. This unfortunately carries over in their revelation of who God is, and they end up even feeling forsaken by Him. It is because they haven't had a true example of what love is. The only way to know what true love really is and how it is defined is to receive a revelation of Abba God.

The Bible tells us that God is love: *"He that loveth not knoweth not God; for God is love"* (1 John 4:8). So if God is love, then let's look at love's definition and characteristics to better understand Abba's love for you and how He will treat you.

I certainly understand for many, as we continue to reveal Abba, that love is an awesome attribute to consider. While yet, for some, the revelation of Him may be hard to comprehend or even difficult to receive. This can be as a result of their experience with their earthly father—for better or for worse. And this is especially true if there was no father figure they can relate to or if there was harshness and abuse from that father figure, making it difficult to receive God as Abba or as love. However, if we will take but a moment to see what love is and how it describes our awesome heavenly Daddy, we can see Him for who He really is, and even erase the memories of hurtful experiences.

In fact, First Corinthians 13 shows the true heart and characteristics that not only Christians should emulate but the character and love traits of our heavenly Abba! Remember that God is love so these descriptions are who He is and who He will be in your life! For example, some of the things this chapter defines love as can compare to the traits of Abba. Here are a few examples taken from First Corinthians 13:

- His love endures.

- He is patient.

- He is not envious or boils over in jealousy.

- He is not boastful, haughty, conceited, rude, unmannerly, or prideful.

- He is not selfish, self-seeking, touchy, or resentful.

- He doesn't hold grudges, and He always forgives.

- He believes the best about us and His love never fails.

So we can see from a few of these examples how God will treat us out of His character of love for us. My prayer is that you have begun to see Abba revealed to you in a greater measure. If anyone would ask, so what does He look like? Well, He looks a lot like love; for He is love.

You will be able to answer this with confidence: "He is full of love that never changes, and is faithful, longing to communicate with us. He keeps His eye on us at all times, caring for our every need. He is available to us at all hours of the day because He doesn't sleep or slumber. My heavenly Father is so intimately acquainted with me that He has engraved an image of me on the palm of His hands. He knows how many hairs are upon my head and provides for my every need. He knew me before I was born, declaring that I am fearfully and wonderfully made. There is no ugly with Him. He is so faithful and never changes."

Are you beginning to see Him yet? It is His desire to reveal Himself as Abba to you. Let's continue our journey as we unfold the chapters before us and continue to receive a revelation of Him!

It's time to run to Him! Are you ready for Him to be revealed in your life? We will examine who He is as we take a journey through Scripture and reveal Him in a greater way throughout the remainder of this book! I know it will cause your heart to cry out, "Abba, Father!"

Notes

1. This article can be found on David Alsobrook's website: http://www.davidalsobrook.com.

2. See "The Words of Jesus in the Original Aramaic" by Stephen Missick, available at http://www.davidalsobrook.com.

Chapter Three

Rescuing the Children of Abba

Unto Adam also and to his wife did the Lord
God make coats of skins, and clothed them
(Genesis 3:21).

Watching intensely in the Garden of Eden and studying this newly created being called man, a devilish plan was being plotted in the heart of the enemy. Curiosity flooded this fallen angel named Lucifer, also called Satan. *What is it about these two beings?* he thought. *Why is God acting uniquely different with them? What is all the excitement over Adam and Eve?* He keenly noticed so much time and attention were being given to these born from the very image of God. A seed of jealously was deposited within him and taking root.

Jealous of Abba's Children

But what was more alarming to this ruler of darkness was that God was acting differently than usual. Differently, you say?

Yes, God was acting uniquely different then He had toward anything He had created before these two showed up. He showed them a special love, desire, and intimacy that was never expressed in this manner before. In fact, the angels to this day don't understand the mystery of the gospel or the special love that was demonstrated through Jesus Christ concerning the forgiveness of man's sins. They don't comprehend why God in His love would send His only Son to earth to die on a cross for all mankind (see 1 Pet. 1:12).

Neither do they understand fatherhood as we know it because they haven't experienced the intimacy between Abba and His children. No angel has ever called God Abba as far as the Scriptures reveal. This title is reserved only for His sons and daughters who are created in His image and reconciled back to Him through the Spirit of adoption: *"For ye have not received the spirit of bondage again to fear; but ye have received the Spirit of adoption, whereby we cry, Abba, Father"* (Rom. 8:15). This is why our relationship with God is so special, unique, and different than any other thing created. We are truly in a class of our own because we are children of our heavenly Father!

Why then did Lucifer show up in the Garden of Eden? It was because he hated God's strong desire for a family and the fact that the Lord shared a deep love and communion with His children. The Bible explains the story of Abba's desire for a family and reveals the lengths to which He went to obtain this family through Jesus. He wanted a family so much that He even created the earth as a home for them, placing them in the Garden of Eden to continue this family on earth. Isaiah declares,

> *For thus saith the Lord that created the heavens; God Himself that formed the earth and made it; He hath established it, He created it not in vain, He formed it*

to be inhabited: I am the Lord; and there is none else (Isaiah 45:18).

When God made Adam, He made a son that started the first earthly family (see Luke 3:38) and a race of sons and daughters in Adam (see Gen. 5:1).

Lucifer despised this desire for family and the mere fact that he wasn't created in the same image of God that the human race was. He became jealous of how God was acting toward this species and how they possessed something he didn't. Jealousy set into him because he was full of pride and wanted to be worshipped more than God. He didn't like Adam and Eve worshipping the Lord or God showing love toward His children because he wanted it solely for himself. This is also why he hates our intimate fellowship and love that we have with Abba. It is why he does everything he can to hinder and stop it from flowing in our lives. He wants the praise of men to be his instead of the Lord's.

Lucifer's involvement in the Garden was designed to separate Adam and Eve from God's presence and gain entrance into their lives. He also loathed the fact that Adam and Eve had dominion over the creation and he didn't. So he would wickedly devise a plan to be worshipped by many in the human race and gain the dominion that was given to them alone.

But there was even more to consider in regards to the jealousy of Satan. We know that God wanted to be a heavenly Father and Lucifer recognized now that something was the center of the Lord's attention. God was showing behavior and dialogue that was at a special, unique place than what he had ever experienced. What he couldn't comprehend was how Abba started acting like a heavenly Daddy!

After all, God had a new responsibility and must devote time and attention to His children. This is what a true father does. Think about how parents act once they have children.

They become busy, excited, and completely devoted to their child. They show a range of emotions that is expressed solely to the child they have, often including baby talk that no one understands.

But the devil did not understand the family relationship between God and Adam and Eve. He recognized something had changed and was uniquely different, even testing Adam and Eve in their identity. Lucifer must have overheard conversations between Abba and His children about family, being children of God, and how He was their Father.

This is why he may have said those words in the Garden when he caused Adam and Eve to fall into sin and away from the presence of their heavenly Father. He said, "You will be *like* God, knowing both good and evil" (see Gen. 3:5). The problem was that they already were made in the image of God and in His likeness (see Gen. 1:26). He was tempting them with something they already had and were. Adam and Eve were already like God, they were His son and daughter, and He was their Father. They were created in His image.

This further reveals Lucifer's motive of jealousy toward these children of Abba. He obviously didn't like the fact that they were created in God's image and the family relationship they enjoyed. Lucifer wanted to be like God, he wanted to be like one of the sons of God, but he wasn't created for that purpose and would never be able to relate to Him in that way. This led to his jealousy and hatred toward mankind. It is also why he attacks our walk with God and works hard to keep people from coming to know Abba through Jesus Christ.

Think for a moment about how in today's society, and even throughout history, we know the devil was jealous and angry over God being a Father and having sons and daughters that excluded him. Jesus called the devil the father of lies and a murderer when addressing the religious people: *"Ye are of your father the devil, and the lusts of your father ye will do. He was a murderer from the beginning, and abode not in the truth, because there is no truth in him"* (John 8:44).

Satan murders babies through abortion, he breaks up homes and marriages, he hates the family structure, perverts procreation of men and women through sexual perversion, promotes the falsehood of same-sex marriage and homosexuality, and he helps cause illegitimate children to be born without a father to care or nurture them. He is a murderer and a liar.

Why are all of these at the center of his focus and attacks? It is because Satan hates the family structure and the root of that hatred goes back to the Garden with Adam and Eve. It is found in Lucifer's own jealousy and pride, his hatred of God, especially revealed as Abba, and anyone who accepts and understands sonship with our heavenly Father.

If you notice in all of these acts of sin and pain in the human race and society, they mostly deal with the lack of fathering, parenting, and the family structure that is necessary for healthy, moral living. The root of many of these conditions in men's hearts and society revolves around the fact that man is living without the revelation of a loving God. He is to be known as Abba, a Father to the fatherless. They live without fully comprehending that they are a son or daughter of God through a personal relationship with Jesus Christ. Satan knows this and hates the fact that humans were created to be like God. When he arrogantly announced his evil intent before his fall, he said he wanted to be like the Most High: *"I will ascend above the heights of the clouds; I will be like the most High"* (Isa. 14:14).

This is what the devil hates about us who have given our lives to Jesus and are now new creatures in Christ Jesus. He doesn't like the fact that we are created in God's image, but more importantly, he doesn't like that we are spiritually adopted into the family of Abba. We are special to the Lord and He demonstrates a greater responsibility when we commit ourselves to Him. It is why we shouldn't be afraid, discouraged, or think we are without victory when serving God. We need to hold our chin up high, square our shoulders, and walk with a sense of honor as His beloved children.

The enemy has made it his mission to destroy man—that is important to remember. He works to pervert and break apart the pure image and structure of God the Father and His beloved sons and daughters. Lucifer was jealous over this new creation just as he is of the new creation in Christ. This is because by salvation through Jesus Christ we become reconciled back to our Abba Father as His children and are now called Christians!

A Son Has Fallen

This is why the devil continually watched the interaction between God and Adam and Eve. He took note of their relationship and the way they communicated. He was determined to undermine the Lord and, at all costs, separate this unique relationship. He even made it his mission to attack this family structure and cause it to affect all those who would be born into the earth.

For this to be done, however, the evil serpent would need a plan. What could he do to disrupt this close, intimate bond that God was having with mankind? His strategy would be to attack the family structure just as he does today. In this case, he went after the woman to lure her and then eventually her husband was lured in. If the devil could get them to fall for his satanic plot, the family structure between them and Abba would be greatly affected and cause separation from communion with their heavenly Father. This plan would not just affect them but all generations to come through the centuries, a certain war between Lucifer, Abba, and His sons and daughters.

There would be a continued breaking apart and dividing of families in the earth, dividing them one from another, but especially dividing them from God. If Satan's plan would succeed, then Adam and Eve would no longer have access to their heavenly Daddy as they once had. There would be a barrier between them, and the dynamic of their relationship would be greatly redefined. Better yet, Lucifer knew that if his strategy was successful, he would become the father over those born into the earth, affecting every man's relationship until they were reconciled back to Abba through Jesus Christ.

If Adam and Eve fell for his temptation, then he would become the god of this world and there would be a vast difference between the creation of God and those who would be His reconciled children. How does this take place? It happens because every person born into the earth is still His creation, but not necessarily a spiritual son or daughter of God until they are reconciled back to Abba through Jesus. This reconciliation takes place by accepting Jesus Christ into their hearts and life. Once they commit their lives to Him, then they are reconciled back to their Father. Paul sums it up like this: *"And all things are of God, who hath reconciled us to Himself by Jesus Christ, and hath given to us the ministry of reconciliation"* (2 Cor. 5:18).

It was in the devil's plan to get Adam and Even to fall into sin and bring separation between Abba and His children. He tries the same thing with us today. If he can get us distracted, lure us into sin, and cause us to have a life of heartache and pain, then he can cause that feeling of separation and unworthiness to affect our relationship with our heavenly Father. At all costs, the devil will attempt anything and everything from the moment of our conception, and even before and through our entire life, to interrupt our connection with and our falling in love with Abba.

It is his constant goal to attack family structures. He goes after the different examples of family we see today such as the home and the church family. Whatever he can do to cause us to be separated from our heavenly Daddy, he will find a way to do it. He will put lies into the minds of people about the true nature and character of God, making the Lord out to be a liar and discredit His love, care, and relationship with us. He will use every negative example in our lives of those that have hurt us, angered us, and caused our lives to struggle in order to get us to blame God or think that He is somehow angry with us.

The enemy constantly works to divide our home that we grew up in by causing us to be victims of divorce, abuse, and experience a life without a father, to name but a few. If he can't successfully break apart our home life, he waits for our teenage years to get us off track by rebellion and a life without our heavenly Father. If that doesn't work, he strategizes to divide our marriage, our children, and family to get us to harden ourselves against the Lord, so we no longer walk with Him or serve Him. This is intended to make us disconnect from Abba while looking for things to cover our nakedness, much like Adam and Eve did when they covered themselves with fig leaves.

We often do the same as we try to cover our own hurt and suffering. If the devil can't use this kind of scenario I have described, he will use the love of this world and all it has to offer to get us off track and lose our focus. He will crowd our hearts and minds with all of the pleasures of this earth so we don't find the room in our hearts and lives for Abba. Think how true this is today with more and more people who don't attend church, read their Bibles, pray, or have any real interest in serving God. If they decide to serve the Lord, it is often on their terms and not according to the Lord's standard. Their walk with God is casual at best and lacks the daily passionate pursuit of one who really knows who Abba is. This is why, since the time of this event in the Garden of Eden with Adam and Eve, Satan was strategically working with hatred to affect those who are born in the earth. He doesn't want the heavenly Father and His creation to be reconciled to one another. He wants to continue to cause separation with Abba and the people of this earth.

Think for a moment what it must have been like as Adam and Eve disobeyed the Lord by listening to that cunning serpent. Satan was celebrating his apparent victory and sneering as he watched them clothe themselves with fig leaves, hiding from the presence of God. A son had fallen and the devil was enjoying his well-calculated plot. He had humans right where he wanted them and wanted nothing more than to cause hurt in the heart of Abba over His fallen children.

Yet, what the devil didn't know was that God had a plan too. Their sin didn't take the Lord by surprise and He would not be outmaneuvered or outsmarted. This devilish plan would certainly redefine man's relationship with God, but it would also cause a son to fall! Yes, a son would fall, not just Adam and Eve, but all mankind would be part of this fallen race through sin.

It was as if the words, "A son has fallen," echoed a cry throughout all the earth and permeated everything that had been created. You could hear the reverberating sound, "A son has fallen; a son has fallen." I wonder, did all of Heaven stand back to see what Abba would do? Did hell and its entire demonic hosts sneer with a sense of satisfaction? Abba, saddened but not taken by surprise, already had a plan way before the foundations of this earth were made, and way before Adam and Eve ever sinned: *"According as He hath chosen us in Him before the foundation of the world, that we should be holy and without blame before Him in love"* (Eph. 1:4).

This plan would involve a member of the heavenly family to save this earthly family He had made and all mankind forever. He would have to offer a Son for His now lost sons. This is exactly the heavenly plan that the devil didn't account for when he attacked the family structure the Lord had created. God would offer a plan for His fallen children, a plan that works for any family or person ever divided, broken, being a victim, or separated from God by sin. His Son offered to reconcile humanity back to their God. It was a plan that would rescue the lost sons and daughters of Abba forever!

Rescuing the Children of Abba

We sometimes forget that God is truly for us and can handle anyone or anything coming against us. He is so incredibly in love with us and spilled His own blood to prove it. But the enemy still tries to convince us that God doesn't care or that He chooses to be good to some and hands out heartaches and tragedies to others. The devil points his finger to those who have failed and hurt us in our lives as well. As a result, he is quick to say, "See, God will fail you too."

Satan works our entire life to get us to second-guess God's Word, love, and intentions toward us. He convinces some that it all depends on the day and the mood God is in that determines if and when He will show goodness to us. But we must always remember Abba's love for us is greater than we can comprehend, and His faithfulness lasts for thousands of generations. How do we know this is true? We know because of His plan. He has our back!

We must never forget for a moment that God has our back. I remember when I was going through some challenging times where it seemed as if it was one attack after another and I just wanted to give up. Yet God spoke to me and said, "Don't you give up, son; not for a moment. I have your back and will defend you. You will see My goodness and faithfulness. Now rest in Me and My Word!"

Praise God the same is true for you too! God has your back! We can see this by His plan to rescue the lost sons and daughters of Abba when Adam and Eve fell that day in sin and from the presence of God. He had their back because He is a committed Father, both to them and to us all that would be born throughout time, even if we would hate and reject Him.

This marvelous plan God had before sin entered the world was to get His sons and daughters back, reconciled with Him again. This was so He could be their Father and they His children with nothing missing and nothing broken between them. This is why, when Jesus came into the earth as a baby, it was announced by the angel Gabriel, "Peace on earth and goodwill toward men" (see Luke 2:14). God was sending His answer to bring His creation back to Himself through sonship! Nothing would be missing or broken in this relationship because Jesus would pay the full price for all mankind! This plan, right from the moment of man's original sin, was to get His beloved sons and daughters back into right fellowship with Him.

If humanity would have consequences and punishment for their sin, God offered a solution that revealed His great love. We often think that when God cursed the man, the woman, and the earth (see Gen. 4), that He was some mean ole nasty Father punishing His children, and that is the way He always is and will be toward us. Yes, there were righteous actions He had to take because of their sinful choice to disobey Him. But He was also instructing them according to the results of their sins and what it had now done to them and the earth.

God disciplines us, and, yes, there are consequences for our sin—there always are and always will be. We know that the best life the Bible tells us to live is one that is pure and striving to live holy before God and man. And we must never forget that the wages of sin is death (see Rom. 6:23). This means we need to come out from living like the world and serve God in honor and purity, set apart from the evils of our day. This is always the way God desires it, as it is for our own benefit that we do this.

What reveals God's love to us in the midst of Adam and Eve's sin is the fact that He offered a plan to fallen man, showing His heart as Abba, not just our Creator! The only option was to offer His only Son to return all of His sons and daughters back to Him. This plan was spoken of as a mystery to the devil: *"And I will put enmity between thee and the woman, and between thy seed and her seed; it shall bruise thy head, and thou shalt bruise his heel"* (Gen. 3:15).

Had the devil known, he wouldn't have crucified the Lord of glory. If he crucified Jesus, then God would have access to His creation as their Father once again. This would be available to all mankind if they would return to God and call upon His Son to be saved. This would also allow them to be brought back into His heavenly family, enabling them to call Him "Abba Father" once again.

Why should God bother with fallen man? It was because He had committed to being a Father to us and abandoning us would be an unjust crime. So through His righteousness and justice, He had to show that He had always had a dedication and commitment to the well-being of humankind as their Father. This is why He had to have a plan to rescue His lost sons and daughters from sin and the devil.

Again, this is reflected in the sending and promising of His own Son, Jesus, to die for the sins of all humanity. We must remember that when Adam and Eve sinned, all mankind and the earth became enslaved to the devil, death, and sin. However, God immediately intervened by promising to send Jesus, who would redeem man and deliver them from their sins. He came to the earth to reveal His Father and return us to our heavenly Abba through reconciliation.

He commissioned His disciples to reach people by going into the entire world and telling them of the good news of the salvation of His heavenly plan that wasn't just offered to Adam and Eve, but to everyone in the earth. He offered to forgive man of their sins and bring the heart of Daddy back to His creation through forgiveness. It would give mankind the opportunity to return to Him as sons and daughters in His Kingdom. This is why God tells those of us who are Christians to go and reach people—to reveal the love and heart of Abba, sharing with them God's eternal desire to be their heavenly Father. God so longs to have His sons and daughters come home and be with Him for all eternity that He would rescue them at all costs, offering the spilling of His Son's blood through the cross.

I already mentioned that God has our back and had a plan in place before the world was even formed. He offered the back of Jesus—in fact, His whole body would be beaten, whipped, bruised, bloodied, spit upon, and nailed to a wooden cross—to prove that He has our back! Why did He do this? A son had fallen, but not just *a* son, but the whole human race born into the earth was separated and fallen from their heavenly Creator and Father.

This is why this marvelous plan would provide a removal of our sins and offer forgiveness to those who would call upon His name. This plan of Abba was greater than the enemy's strategy and was manifested when Jesus came to seek and save lost men in order to bring them back to their God (see Luke 19:10).

Abba's Covering

It is so beautiful and comforting to know that God had a plan that concerned you, me, and the entire human race throughout eternity. He is a good and faithful Father. His love is so great that even when Adam and Eve sinned, His heart as our heavenly Daddy was revealed. He put His arms around them and showed that He was committed to them. He not only promised His Son in the plan of redemption He made, but put His arms of love upon them by animal coats of skins: *"Unto Adam also and to his wife did the Lord God make coats of skins, and clothed them"* (Gen. 3:21).

You might be thinking, *How could that be God's arms of love upon His children?* Well, in order to understand this we must recognize what these coats of skins represented and why God chose to cover them this way. It was a prophetic act and fore-shadowing of salvation through the shed blood of Jesus Christ. Again, it was His act of love, a covering of His hands upon them and the entire future human race. He did this to cover their sin and shame, or what would later be called a blood aton-ing for their sins (see Lev. 16:34). We need to also realize today that Abba puts His love upon us in the same way, except this time it is by the Lamb of God who takes away the sins of the world and covers the nakedness and the shame of our sins, for Jesus is *"the Lamb of God, which taketh away the sin of the world"* (John 1:29).

How does He take our sins away? He does it just as He did with the animal skins that He provided for Adam and Eve in the Garden. He provides His love and forgiveness through Jesus's shed blood upon the cross. This means whenever we sin, we can ask our Abba to forgive us and He will be faithful and just to forgive us of our sins and cleanse us from all unrigh-teousness (see 1 John 1:9). Just as He covered them that day, He covers us through the blood of Jesus and forgives us, accepts us, cleanses us, affirms us, and puts His loving arms around us to help us!

This is what the coats of skins represented—they showed once again that the heart of Abba is revealed in dealing with the sin of Adam and Eve. God was showing that in His love

He would provide the first and last sacrifice needed to redeem man from sin. You see, when they both sinned, they fell short of the glory of God and lost His presence. There would now be a separation between them and Abba because of the sinful act they committed.

But what would Abba do? He begins by covering them with these coats of skin to reveal His faithfulness and love to them. He follows by telling them the consequences of their sinful actions as any loving father would and should do to his children (see Gen. 4). He then continues by explaining to them what life will be like now that they have disobeyed Him and how this would even change their relationship with Him in the future. He goes on to tell them of the cursed earth, the soil, the pain of childbearing, and sweating from the brow in a life of work and labor. All of this is far short of what Abba had originally intended, but man was given a choice: would they choose to honor their heavenly Father or not? After all, nothing takes God by surprise, and though this choice was given, it would show if they would want Him as their Father by honoring Him. There had to be a free will choice to determine the relationship and what level of involvement they would allow of God in their lives.

In His love, God doesn't leave them to be lost in their shame from their sinful actions. Abba does something a true dad will always do. Rather than condemn, cast them off, and make them feel degraded, He puts His love upon them like a father putting his arm around his child who is struggling or has done something wrong, thus the reason He put animal skins upon them immediately after they sinned.

These coats of skins would forever represent something powerful to come. First, they would restore the feeling of love and acceptance by Abba. This is because before they sinned, they were both clothed with His wonderful presence. However, now after they sinned, they were naked and ashamed, thus the reason for making fig leaves to hide their shame (see Gen. 3:8-10). The coats of skins that God the Father provided would restore that covering of His presence through what would later become animal sacrifices for the atoning of Israel's sins.

It would make sense then for these animal coats that were provided to Adam and Eve to be dripping in blood, and they would provide a temporary covering for their sins until God's only begotten Son would die by shedding His blood for all. He would do this as the Lamb of God who would take away the sins of the world and rescue all the lost created children of Abba. They revealed Abba's love, grace, and covering.

I want you to be encouraged that in the same way that God showed His love to Adam and Eve, He will show His love and forgiveness to you as well. This is why when we sin, make mistakes, and feel like we have failed God, He is there to wrap His love and arms around us, bringing us back to Him. You are not a failure or so bad that He can't find you or forgive your sins. You are a child of Abba and He is never without His love to cleanse you and restore you, making you better than you were before or ever could be.

Examples of Abba's Covering

There are several examples in the Scripture that reveal the Lord's love and covering, and His forgiveness and care for our lives through garments, like the animal skins on Adam and Eve.

Polluted in blood:

In Ezekiel 16, we see a beautiful prophetic picture of God providing forgiveness of sin and rescuing the lost children of Abba. As the chapter reveals, we were all polluted in our blood because of Adam's sin and as a result we all carry the same sin nature. This means that anyone born into the earth would be a carrier of this polluted blood of sin. And it is why Jesus had to be born of a virgin and had to shed His blood for the polluted sinful blood of the lost children of Abba.

Yet this chapter in Ezekiel reveals God passing by in His love and commanding polluted blood to live or, better yet, revealing the forgiveness of sins through Jesus. God said through Ezekiel, *"And when I passed by thee, and saw thee polluted in thine own blood, I said unto thee when thou wast in thy blood, Live; yea, I said unto thee when thou wast in thy blood, Live"* (Ezek. 16:6).

As we further read in Ezekiel, we see the same prophetic picture like we did with the animal coats of skins that God used as a covering for Adam and Eve. God is seen putting His garment upon Jerusalem but, in addition, it is prophetic for both Jew and Gentile being offered salvation and the New Covenant through Jesus and His shed blood:

> *Now when I passed by thee, and looked upon thee, behold, thy time was the time of love; and I spread My skirt over thee, and covered thy nakedness: yea, I sware unto thee, and entered into a covenant with thee, saith the Lord God, and thou becamest Mine* (Ezekiel 16:8).

This is once again a beautiful picture of what happened the day Adam and Eve sinned and became polluted in their sin and their blood. It also shows all of mankind in the same condition—in need of a Savior! In both examples, it represents Abba providing a covering of love and forgiveness, reconciling them back to Himself!

The coat of Joseph:

The coat of many colors given to Joseph by his father, Jacob, is also a wonderful example of a covering (see Gen. 37:3).

Joseph's brothers were jealous of this coat and the favor he had with his father, so they threw Joseph in a pit when he came to check on them one day. They then took his coat and made it look like Joseph died. They did this by killing a goat and dipping the coat in its blood. Then they took the bloody coat to their father.

> And they took Joseph's coat, and killed a kid of the goats, and dipped the coat in the blood; and they sent the coat of many colours, and they brought it to their father; and said, This have we found: know now whether it be thy son's coat or no (Genesis 37:31-32).

Once again, this reveals Abba to us today. How? This is because much like Joseph, God gave us a coat of blessing and favor. It was in His image that we were created and this caused us to possess tremendous favor. Yet, we were hated, despised, and left for dead in the pit of sin and despair, being destined to the pit of hell.

It can also be likened to some who may have been mistreated and lied about, much like Joseph was, and feel as though they did nothing wrong. In other words, life hasn't been fair and some people are victims of others' unfair actions, especially those of family or loved ones. However, like the animal skins God provided in the Garden, this coat of Joseph's, dripping in blood, prophetically reveals today that no matter what pit we are in, what lie that has been spoken about us, or what has been done to us, a way has been provided out of the pit of hell and despair. It is through the shed blood of Jesus, which is the coat we wear as Christians, that proves we have been forgiven of our sins. It shows that we now belong to Abba through Jesus's shed blood, and the enemy no longer has power over us!

We are now wearing spiritual robes of righteousness, called by God and known as the righteousness of God in Christ Jesus. No matter our sin or shame, we have been provided a covering, a washing away of our sins forever. God has put His arms around us and we are loved and accepted by Him!

Noah and the garment to cover his shame:

The Bible tells us of how Noah, after the flood, began drinking of the grapes of the earth and became drunk. One of his three sons, Ham, saw Noah's nakedness, and went and told his two brothers, Shem and Japheth. Rather than exposing Noah's nakedness and partaking of sin, they graciously walked backward, covering their father's nakedness: *"And Shem and Japheth took a garment, and laid it upon both their shoulders, and went backward, and covered the nakedness of their father; and their faces were backward, and they saw not their father's nakedness"* (Gen. 9:23).

This act of covering was vital to all of us; the reason being was because it was through Abraham, who was part of a later lineage of Shem, that the Israelites were chosen to be the sons of Abba. It was this same lineage through Shem and Abraham that the Messiah would come to provide the ultimate covering of the nakedness of our sins—the shedding of His blood.

In the same way, we might have made mistakes like Noah did or really sinned, making a mess and embarrassment of our lives. Perhaps we know those like Ham who have made it their mission to let everyone know what we have done or the kind of person we have become. Yet in the midst of it all, Abba has clothed our nakedness, past life, and shame through His Son. We are covered, forgiven, and offered a new and abundant life in Christ! This is how Abba has rescued the lost sons!

To further illustrate Abba's love for you and me, there is yet another example that Jesus tells in Scripture that directly relates to how God revealed His love to Adam and Eve with the coats of skin and how He shows His love to us today. The story of the prodigal son we find another encouraging example of our heavenly Father's love for us, especially when we miss it. It shows His intense pursuit of us, wrapping His arms of love around us, and not letting us go. We are truly special to Him!

Running to Abba

In the story of the prodigal son that Jesus told in Luke 15, we see a son who becomes wayward and lost after he leaves his family. He lives his life separate from his family, without a father figure for a part of his life. He continues to try to fill the emptiness of his heart but to no avail; and after realizing it has cost him everything, including his family and most importantly his father, he desires to return home. This sounds like a lot of people today, doesn't it? Yet, what is this young prodigal son to do? So in the midst of his broken life he decides to return to his father. Jesus tells this portion of the story like this:

> *And when he came to himself, he said, How many hired servants of my father's have bread enough and to spare, and I perish with hunger! I will arise and go to my father, and will say unto him, Father, I have sinned against heaven, and before thee* (Luke 15:17-18).

It is why the animal coats dripping with blood can be further understood to prophetically signify how they reveal Abba in this story. This wayward son represents all the created sons of our heavenly Father who have wandered from Him into their own lives of sin and lasciviousness. It wasn't until he came to the end of himself and repented that he returned home. He is not sure what to expect, but decides to go back and be reconciled to his father.

As he is returning, however, he sees his father off in the distance. Once the father, who represents Abba in the story, sees his lost son, he runs to meet him, falling upon his neck, kissing him.

And he arose, and came to his father. But when he was yet a great way off, his father saw him, and had compassion, and ran, and fell on his neck, and kissed him. And the son said unto him, Father, I have sinned against heaven, and in thy sight, and am no more worthy to be called thy son (Luke 15:20-21).

What an amazing picture of lost sons and daughters returning to the loving arms of Abba after realizing life without Him is unfulfilling and nothing worth celebrating. Look for a moment at the awesome love, compassion, forgiveness, and acceptance our God has for us. He went running after His children! Are you kidding me? God *ran* to us—I can hardly believe it myself. Yet this is exactly what Jesus revealed in the nature of Abba in this story. God was doing the pursuing, all it took was for the son to decide life without Him was empty, meaningless, and nobody loved him like his heavenly Father. Once you make that decision in your heart, look out, because you will hear His footsteps, the heavenly pursuit of God almighty, your loving Creator and Abba, running with His arms wide open to receive you.

It's amazing how He reaches out for us even when we have done wrong and gone our own way. Incredibly, we see an even deeper revelation of God's heart toward us in the loving action we see the father do after hugging his lost son. He immediately puts a garment upon him and celebrates his return: *"But the father said to his servants, Bring forth the best robe, and put it on him; and put a ring on his hand, and shoes on his feet* (Luke 15:22).

Oh, what joy; what celebration in Heaven when one sinner repents! What jubilation when you and I finally decided we wanted God in our lives, returning to our Father through salvation in Jesus Christ. What excitement in all of Heaven and the smile upon the face of our Abba when we finally call out to Him! He is exactly like the father Jesus is describing in this story. He is full of such happiness, celebrating our return.

It is exciting to know that the robe put on this prodigal son is again the exact same prophetic picture of the awesome plan of God and the animal skins that covered Adam and Eve after they sinned. And in much the same way, this son was covered by Abba and rescued from a life apart from Him!

Abba's Kiss

What is so touching about the story Jesus told, revealing Abba to us, are those amazing actions our heavenly Father has toward His people. This father, like God, responded when seeing his son returning. Not only did he run to him, but the Scripture tells us that he fell on his son's neck and repeatedly kissed him (see Luke 15:20).

Think for a moment about that kiss! It is our heavenly Daddy's kiss to all the wayward sons and daughters of creation. This kind of affection is not just reserved for lost sinners, but is the very heart and being of God our Father. He is not afraid, ashamed, or reserved about showing us His love and affection. We just need to reach for Him and pursue Him every day of our lives. And, in response, He showers us with affection and mercy.

This kind of expression is not understood by the casual of heart who seek God on a whim or without being totally sold out to Him. It is not comprehended by those who continue to live a life of sin, knowing it separates them from enjoying a pure, fulfilled life with God. Nor is it often obtained by the uncommitted and unfaithful of heart who fail in a daily pursuit of God through His Scriptures, involvement in the Kingdom, and a life of prayer. If we want God, we must express our desire to Him through what we do. When God knows we are committed and we truly want Him, then He lavishes us with His kisses and love in return.

God can't help Himself, for it is His nature to bless us abundantly just like the father did with the wayward son. He said,

> *Bring forth the best robe, and put it on him; and put a ring on his hand, and shoes on his feet: and bring hither the fatted calf, and kill it; and let us eat, and be merry: for this my son was dead, and is alive again; he was lost, and is found. And they began to be merry* (Luke 15:22-24).

What does this mean for you and me? It means Abba has rescued us from the hand of our enemy. We were lost, but now we are found. We need to let Him kiss us with the kisses of His love, affirmation, and acceptance. We are now clothed with His love, grace, and forgiveness. It is our honor and expression of our love to walk pure before Him and seek Him daily. He is faithful to us, and now we must be faithful to Him. It's time to run to our Abba! Are you ready? I know I am!

We have an incredible heavenly Father who is just waiting for us! Yes, He is waiting, watching, running, and pursuing us in return. Watch out for His kisses of love! They will fall upon you as He puts His loving arms around you and lavishes you with His love. You won't regret it and won't ever want to come out of His loving arms again. After all, why should we when Abba's kiss of love is like no other?

Chapter Four

He Is God and Abba

My Father is God and I will exalt Him
(Exodus 15:2 personal paraphrase).

The heart of the Lord was full of excitement. It was now the time to approach this once pagan man, a worshipper of the sun, named Abram. Abba had been watching him intensely. He had spoken to this man a few times, looking to him for something special that would carry a unique plan throughout the earth. It was something that would affect nations and generations to come, even us in our day and time. It would carry Heaven's mystery and bring all the lost created sons and daughters of Abba back to Him. God waited for this moment in Abram's life to make His more formal introduction, even though the Lord had spoken certain things to him before. Yet, this time it would be a serious moment for God to introduce Himself and reveal His plan to Abram, even changing his name to Abraham (see Gen. 17:5).[1]

God would need this earthly man to agree to a covenant relationship with Him, being part of the strategy to bring forth the promised Son of God who would save all the families of the earth. Of course, God knew the outcome before He even initiated the response. Yet it was still in the hands of this man to choose. Would he open his heart and life to continue the plan God unveiled in the Garden of Eden with Adam and Eve? Or would he choose to follow his own path, doing his own will throughout his lifetime? This plan had been carefully calculated by the Lord and needed someone who would agree and submit to the heart and desire of the Lord for it to be carried out. He would choose Abraham. But why him?

Abraham and Abba

God has always used people in the earth throughout history—very rarely acting by Himself without a human agent to work through. Yet Abraham had unique traits the Lord was looking for in this world to become what the Scripture calls "the father of us all" (see Rom. 4:16). He would give his life to God, and in return the Lord would make him the earthly father that would bring a restoration of the family of God in the earth. Abba had searched for a friend that He could choose to start this family and that would help to rescue His lost creation. They would help carry the royal seed of God into the earth, bringing forth God's Son as the promised Messiah, reconciling mankind back to Him.

But how does God do this? He needs a friend who would obey Him completely. Watching, He liked what He saw in Abraham. The Lord came to him in a vision, introducing Himself as his shield and provider. Abraham responded to the Lord's introduction as his provider by asking Him what He would give him since he was an old man now and childless.

After these things the word of the Lord came unto Abram
in a vision, saying, Fear not, Abram: I am thy shield,
and thy exceeding great reward. And Abram said, Lord

God, what wilt Thou give me, seeing I go childless, and
the steward of my house is this Eliezer of Damascus?
(Genesis 15:1-2)

You could say that was a smart answer from Abraham, don't you think? After all, if God introduced Himself to us in a vision, stating He was our provider like this experience, I am sure we would be quick to ask something that was dear to us as well. This is exactly what Abraham does. He wanted a son while Abba wanted all mankind that He had created to return to Him as their God and Father personally.

Can you imagine this scene? Two fathers, one a heavenly Daddy wanting a family on earth and the other, Abraham, wanting an earthly family. They were a perfect match to enter into an agreement in order to bring to fruition what both of them deeply desired in their hearts. Yet, it wouldn't be easy. God would need Abraham to obey and Abraham would need God to help him. This was because Abraham was about 90 years old and without God's help he couldn't produce a child.

Something so amazing and so heavenly begins to transpire as God and Abraham enter a covenant agreement to bring forth this heavenly plan. The word *covenant* simply means "an agreement with a person or group of people to whom you are deeply committed." God was committed—He just needed a man in the earth that would be committed as well!

The sky became dark and God came to show Abraham who He was. He required him to make a blood sacrifice by dividing specific animals, including cutting an ox in half (see Gen. 15:9-10). Why would this be necessary? Remember the coats of skin Abba provided for Adam and Eve? The Bible calls them *coats* of skin (plural, meaning more than one). It would be obvious to conclude that there were two of them, one for Adam and one for Eve, symbolizing God's plan of redemption through the shed blood of Jesus.

Now Abraham would be part of this plan, but a covenant would have to be made and not broken between God and Abraham. Once these animals were divided and their blood dripping on the ground, Abraham fell into a deep sleep and the Lord appeared. He appeared to Abraham as a smoking furnace and a burning light; and He walked through the two halves of the animal sacrifice (see Gen. 15:17).

What an amazing love God displayed here! He was entering into a covenant agreement with man. He was counting on him to be part of this heavenly plan of reconciliation; a plan that would bless mankind and restore Abba's creation back to Himself, only if they would call upon Him through Jesus.

Those two halves are another demonstration of Abba reaching out to lost man, reminding us of the animal coats of skin; but even more so, we must never forget His Son, Jesus, hanging as the Lamb of God, fulfilling the ultimate plan of God by shedding His own blood on the cross. And this blood is applied to our lives to bring forgiveness of sins. Jesus was crucified between two thieves, thus the reason for the animals divided with Abraham. It represented the covenant that God made with Abraham and a New Covenant being made with all mankind. Jesus's blood was spilled, very similar to this moment God was having with Abraham. Jesus paid the price for us so we could enter into covenant with God the Father. What happened on the cross was the fulfillment of the prophetic foreshadowing between God and Abraham entering into a blood covenant together with these animals divided in half!

We must also not forget Israel's crossing of the Red Sea when it comes to covenants. The sea was divided in two and, in addition, there was also a cloud of smoke and fire that followed them. In all of these examples, we can conclude that we have an amazing heavenly Daddy that went to great lengths to rescue all humanity, if they would but receive Him. Foreshadowed throughout the Bible was an awesome covenant plan that had to be wisely calculated by God to bring His return into the lives of all peoples to be their heavenly Father again!

Yet, in the midst of all of this, why was Abraham chosen? It was because the focus of God's heart was for a family. He lost the family of mankind in the Garden of Eden by their choice to disobey Him and listen to the voice of the enemy. But Abba wouldn't give up. He pursued Abraham, and all Abraham needed to do was agree with God's plan!

How would this happen? Remember, God and Abraham entered into an agreement together. They both entered into covenant and they both would agree to the terms and conditions. It would require a Son for a son. God would have to offer His Son for all mankind and Abraham would have to be willing to give his son, Isaac, to carry out the earthly plan.

God needed a covenant man whom He could enter into a personal relationship with. This covenant relationship would be mutually agreed upon. God would offer Abraham everything He had, including Himself and the future promise of His Son for the whole world through his seed. In return, Abraham was to give Abba everything he owned, including his only son, Isaac, to carry out this plan.

But there is still an important part of this covenant relationship that had to be fulfilled if it was truly agreed upon—the Lord would ask something so heart-wrenching and close to the very heart of Abraham. God would ask him to take his son, Isaac, the promised child whom he waited for 24 years to be born, and sacrifice him on the altar. *Are you serious?* you're probably wondering. *Who would sacrifice their own son, especially if it was your only son you waited so long for? What was God thinking?*

And he said, Take now thy son, thine only son Isaac, whom thou lovest, and get thee into the land of Moriah;

and offer him there for a burnt offering upon one of the mountains which I will tell thee of (Genesis 22:2).

However, this didn't phase Abraham one bit because he was committed to obeying the Lord in whatever He asked in order to fulfill this covenant plan of God. He was full of faith and fully persuaded of what God was asking of him. Abraham even told his servants that he was going to worship the Lord, offer his only son, Isaac, as a sacrifice, and then return again: *"And Abraham said unto his young men, Abide ye here with the ass; and I and the lad will go yonder and worship, and come again to you"* (Gen. 22:5).

What faith, what trust, and what obedience. No wonder God chose this man to be the vessel to use to fulfill His purpose in the earth. This is what God was looking for concerning Abraham. You see, if God would require Abraham to give his only son, then Abba would have to give His only begotten Son, Jesus, to be sacrificed as well in the fullness of time. This was the agreement that was made; it required mutual obedience. What was required of the one would be required and asked of the other!

This is why God would choose this man, Abraham, for such an awesome act of love and obedience. The only reason Abba would make such a demand of him was not because of His desire to see a man kill his son, but because He would need someone in the earth to give Him legal access to work through. This would enable Him to work through a covenant agreement to help get *all* of the created sons and daughters of Abba back through Jesus Christ. He would merely need someone to have His heart, someone who would reveal His desire to give everything, including his son, to pay the ultimate price for sin. Abraham was the man that would do this. He was the very one that God had His eyes upon to carry out this plan.

This was no small thing. It required the right choice, the right person to have a heart of faith and obedience. You see, if Abraham, a devoted father, would be willing to give his son in this covenant agreement, then Abba would have to be willing to give His Son as well; and that is exactly what happened! We see what God saw in Abraham, a heart of faith and obedience, as we carefully look at Abraham the day he took Isaac to be sacrificed:

> *And Abraham took the wood of the burnt offering, and laid it upon Isaac his son; and he took the fire in his hand, and a knife; and they went both of them together* (Genesis 22:6).

This can be prophetically compared with the account the apostle John mentions in his writings of Jesus carrying His cross to Golgotha (see John 19:17). It is a prophetic parallel between Abraham and Isaac as we read in Genesis 22:6, and Abba and Jesus in John 19. In both examples, it was a father and son going together to offer a sacrifice. It is an incredible revelation of God's love to us. So just how is this connected?

It was Abraham's son, Isaac, who bore the wood of his own sacrifice upon his back just like Abba's Son would carry a wooden cross on His back. Abraham and Isaac were united together in carrying the wood for a sacrifice, and so was God the Father and Jesus. In fact, it mentions that both Abraham and Isaac went together: *"and they went both of them together"* (Gen. 22:6).

This is exactly what happened when Jesus carried His cross to the place He was to be crucified. It was He and Abba together. It was Father and Son together as Jesus carried His cross, offering the ultimate and final sacrifice for all people! In this amazing act of love and fulfilling the plan of God, you see the revealing of Abba's heart and character. Jesus carried the wooden cross on His back that was put on Him by Abba; and

Isaac carried the wood on his back that put on him by Abraham. In both examples, they were willingly offering their lives as a sacrifice.

Abraham, like we've previously mentioned, would be carefully selected by God to be the father of us all and to help bring this plan into the earth. This is why it was vital that God chose the right person for the job. They had to agree to carry out this plan of our heavenly Daddy concerning all creation.

Again, God was looking for something special in the heart of the person He would choose. He was looking for the faith, love, and obedience Abraham possessed to offer his son. Yet, there was something else here as well. Abraham could willingly obey and offer Isaac according to the covenant terms he agreed to with God because he had character, faith, and a heart that wanted to obey God. What was even more appealing to the Lord was the fact that Abraham had the same qualities and character of a father, which God also possessed. We know this by the characteristics of Abraham according to Genesis 18:19:

> *For I know him, that he will command his children and his household after him, and they shall keep the way of the Lord, to do justice and judgment; that the Lord may bring upon Abraham that which He hath spoken of him.*

What was this something seen by Abba in Abraham, that he would be called the father of us all? Perhaps it was the fact that Abraham would exemplify in the earth a true revealing of the character and nature of God Himself. He would have the characteristics of a dad that would be pleasing to the Lord. This was important because God would need to find a man who would represent a true father, one who would reveal Abba's heart and will in the earth. This is why Abraham was chosen.

Abraham was a family man who would command his children after the ways of the Lord. He would teach them to do what was right before the Lord; he would take the attributes of Abba and share them, living them out before his household and children. No wonder he was chosen and called the father of many nations (see Gen. 17:5).

God had a great love and relationship with Abraham. The Scripture tells us that Abraham was a friend of God, even considering him in the outcome of Sodom and Gomorrah (see Gen. 18). Abraham would be the closest thing in the earth at that time to reveal God more personally to the people. However, even this would be limited until Jesus would be born to reveal Abba at the highest level Israel and those in the earth would ever know and come to understand.

Abba and His Firstborn Son, Israel

God longed to show to mankind more personally and intimately who He was. Yet He would have to wait until Jesus would reveal Him as Abba. However, before this would happen, man knew Him as God. It wasn't until after the covenant He made with Abraham and his descendants that He would be known more as a father figure, corporately speaking, and not yet as a personal heavenly Father.

God, in His desire to be a Father to each person individually, would have to settle upon a corporate relationship and understanding instead. Who would God choose to further carry out His plan to become a Father to a nation, which would lead to His ultimate plan to be known individually as Abba to both Jew and Gentile? He would choose Jacob, the grandson of His covenant man, Abraham, to fulfill His promise to him. God would change Jacob's name to Israel (see Gen. 35:10), and this would continue His promise through Abraham to raise up a mighty nation unto Him (see Gen. 12:2). God chose the man

Israel to become part of this great plan of redemption and a chosen nation. Remember, this is why Abraham was chosen in the first place, and now why Israel was chosen. Through this lineage would come a powerful nation and it would become the corporate son of God, a nation of peoples. They would become what God would call His firstborn son!

Again, this relationship was limited until the price of all mankind would be paid for through Jesus Christ. Then both Jew and Gentile would be collectively engrafted into the promise, having now the awesome opportunity and privilege to be reconciled back to God our Father, calling Him Abba, being one corporate family (see Gal. 3:13-14)! This is why Israel only corporately knew Him and the priests were the mediators between them and God because the price of sin had not yet been paid through Jesus.

God, in His desire to be Abba personally to mankind and gain back His creation, would further carry His covenant plan with the nation of Israel. He would be their God and Father and they would be His firstborn son. What does this mean? It meant that God would be Israel's Father, meaning that He would watch over them, protect them, discipline them, and love them as a nation born from the lineage of Abraham, Isaac, and Jacob. They would be limited in their access to Him, having to go through a mediator to represent them.

This is why Israel knew God as the Father of their nation and why God called Israel His firstborn son: *"And thou shalt say unto Pharaoh, Thus saith the Lord, Israel is My son, even My firstborn"* (Exod. 4:22). And He goes on to reveal to Moses that He would be their Father and take care of them: *"And I will take you to Me for a people, and I will be to you a God"* (Exod. 6:7). Again, this would be limited to knowing Him as God and not yet personally as Abba, our heavenly Father.

The title "firstborn," especially in the Jewish culture, was in reference to those who carried on the family lineage and were given the family rights of inheritance. It was a title given also to Ephraim, David, and our Lord Jesus throughout Scripture. Of course we know Jesus is Abba's only "begotten" Son, meaning He was God coming to the earth in the flesh, carrying this title because He is Lord over all creation and is He is called the "firstborn" (see Col. 1:15).

When the Bible refers to Ephraim, and even David, in certain Scriptures as the firstborn, it was spoken in context of their birthright and their family responsibility. However, when we are discussing Israel as God's firstborn son, we remember this refers to His love and tender affection toward them. This is why Hosea said, *"When Israel was a child, then I loved him, and called My son out of Egypt"* (Hos. 11:1), speaking of the nation of Israel.

The title of firstborn was also in reference to the nation of Israel, which was under the bondage of Pharaoh in Egypt. God the Father wanted to set His son, this nation free. This can be found in the discussion between Moses and Pharaoh concerning the firstborn. If Pharaoh would not let the people go, then his own firstborn son and all those in Egypt—both man and beast—would die because they oppressed and held the firstborn nation of Israel in bondage: *"'Let My son go, so he may worship Me.' But you refused to let him go; so I will kill your firstborn son"* (Exod. 4:23 NIV).

So we come to understand just how much Abba loved the people of Israel because of His love and agreement He had made with Abraham, and that was followed through with Isaac and Jacob. Being the firstborn was an important status given by God because it meant they had great honor and, in the sense of a family, they would receive a double portion of the father's inheritance unless he decided to give it to another son. Whoever was chosen as the firstborn son would receive great favor and respect from the rest of the family.

This was the case with David who later became a king. Even though he would be the youngest child born into the family, he would receive firstborn rights because he was chosen by Abba to become king and the rest of his family would have to honor that status. God said of him:

> *I have found David My servant; with My sacred oil I have anointed him.... He will call out to Me, "You are my Father, my God, the Rock my Savior." I will also appoint him My firstborn, the most exalted of the kings of the earth* (Psalm 89:20, 26-27 NIV).

This didn't mean David was being referenced as firstborn, in the sense of the order in which he was born, but rather in favor and status. In the same way, Israel was corporately chosen by God to be His son. The Lord told Moses that Israel would be His "firstborn" son who would be given great favor, honor, and status from God, even above other nations and peoples. They would be set apart by Him to carry out His plan that would reconcile all men back to Him, to then know Him personally as Abba.

So when God said, "Israel is My firstborn son," He meant they would be granted a close, intimate relationship with God as well as honor from Him, corporately as a nation. What is important to understand, however, in the relationship between Abba and Israel was the fact that even though they were His firstborn son, they didn't know Him as Abba individually but only corporately.

It wasn't until Moses that the idea of a more intimate, personal level with God was even considered. It was only until this time that they began to see a more personal friendship between God and man, as Moses would become a friend of God (see Exod. 33:11).

Moses would still act as a mediator between God and man concerning the nation of Israel. The people would stand at their tents, witnessing God speaking to him from a cloud of His presence and would still need Moses and the priests to represent them before God. The people would still have limited access to Him and would not have personal access to Him except through Moses. It was Moses who talked to God face to face as a man speaks to a friend. Yet, it wasn't as a man speaks to His Abba, or heavenly Father, but as a friend!

I want you to be encouraged to know that God was a Father to the people of Israel corporately and will be one to you personally. We will continue to see Abba revealed through Scripture. As we do, we will understand that even though His plan was limited to being a personal Father in their lives, since the fall of Adam and Eve, this is no longer limited to you and me any longer. We have a personal and complete access to Him as our God and Abba.

In the next chapter we will see how Jesus came to reveal Abba, not corporately but personally, with such intimacy, love, and care for us. So close, in fact, that He knows how many hairs we have and don't have on our heads. He is intimately acquainted in all our ways. This is the difference between those who knew the Lord as God and Father before Jesus and those of us who know God today as Abba because of Jesus. There is no longer any separation that can keep us from knowing God as Abba intimately. And this is why it is important to have two key revelations in our walk with Him to keep us balanced and have a healthy relationship with Him!

He Is God and Abba

God wanted to be known as a personal Father throughout the earth. It helps us to understand His heart in this area. It also reveals to us two needed revelations in our Christian walk that will help us as well. It was the same revelation that He wanted Israel to comprehend—the understanding of who He is as both our God *and* our Father.

Why is it important to understand this? The reason people come to know Him only as the all-powerful God, but not as a loving, intimate, personal heavenly Father, is that all too often people's revelation of the Lord is limited exclusively to knowing God as the powerful, mighty, majestic, righteous God, of which He is. This describes a God who is mighty but often thought of as too strong or fearful to approach. But now that we understand that in many examples in Scripture, when people came in contact with God, they were afraid because He is greater and more powerful than anything they have ever encountered before. Yet, all too often people think He is not approachable or rather moody or temperamental.

This is especially true when people blow it in the Christian walk or feel let down by God. They are then reluctant to run to Him as their Abba but rather hide from Him like Adam and Eve did in the Garden. They stop reading their Bibles, praying, and going to church, believing that God doesn't care about how they feel or their situation. Sometimes people think that this is what they deserve since, after all, He is God and He is out to get them. Some never serve the Lord or come to Him as their Father because someone told them something wrong about the Lord, and they were led to believe that God wouldn't want them because they are so bad. It is because of their lack of understanding Him as a Father that they don't commit their lives to Him or walk with a constant cloud of shame and feelings of abandonment. But when we come to know Him as both God and Father, we will live in the right spiritual, healthy balance that will aid us in our walk with Him.

Yes, God wants us to know that He is God and there is none else besides Him. When He stands up from His throne and comes to the earth, the Scripture tells us that mountains melt like wax at His presence and the earth trembles (see Ps. 97:5). He is certainly the almighty, supreme God and there is no one greater—He is the Most High God. That is not to be argued. Yet what needs to be considered is the fact that He told us to call Him Father. He wants us to know that He is available as a loving Father. And He wants us to understand His tender, compassionate, and personal side; and that is as Abba, our heavenly Daddy.

To illustrate this understanding of Him being both God and Father, we need to look at this from Scriptures. Moses, Miriam, and the people sang a song that signified God's victory over Pharaoh and his army after the Red Sea incident. Notice what they said concerning the Lord: *"My Father is God and I will exalt Him"* (Exod. 15:2, personal paraphrase).

They sang about Him being their Father *and* God. There was a slight problem with Israel's understanding, however. They acknowledged Him as God, in the sense that they sang of His power to give them victory over their enemies and deliver them from Egypt; however, after this song, the Bible tells us in the rest of Exodus 15 that they didn't comprehend Him as Father even though they sang about it. They didn't have a full comprehension of Him in this way. We know this because just three days after singing this song, they were thirsty in the desert without water, which caused them to begin complaining and getting angry with Moses.

> *So Moses brought Israel from the Red sea, and they went out into the wilderness of Shur; and they went three days in the wilderness, and found no water. And when they came to Marah, they could not drink of the waters of Marah, for they were bitter: therefore the name of it was*

> *called Marah. And the people murmured against Moses,*
> *saying, What shall we drink?* (Exodus 15:22-24)

They became bitter in their hearts, forgetting how God had just met their needs through all the miracles three days prior. How quickly they forgot God as the Mighty One; but also how they failed to understand He was their Father. After all, a good father will love them, discipline them, and care for their needs. And this is exactly what God did. He brought them to some bitter water to show them that their heart and attitude were wrong. God then provided for them and their needs, showing that He was committed to caring, loving, and helping them along their way (see Exod. 15:25-27). They just needed to trust Him as their Father.

We can see this important truth from what was mentioned in what they sang. It reveals for us today how to have a healthy relationship with Abba Father. The reason for this is that it shows two necessary distinctions of God's character and personality: First, they sang, *"My Father is..."* This is to know God as our Father, our personal Abba before His other wonderful attributes. Then they continued by singing, *"...is God and I will exalt Him!"* This is different than the first part, which is that He is God. Of course we know He is God, but do we know Him as Father? We understand we can't separate God and Father because they are the same. Yet, in His attributes, He being our Father is more intimate than the revelation of Him being our God.

People mostly have a revelation of a God who is all-powerful, majestic, and mighty, while few have an understanding of Him as their Father. It is usually one or the other, and seldom understood as both. But those who understand Him primarily as God and not as much a Father, often know Him as such, the all-consuming God who answers our prayers by the power of His might. They know and understand Him as God by the fact that He is everywhere and all-powerful. Some even believe He is moody and it depends on what mood we catch Him in if we will receive a blessing or not.

Then there are others who have a revelation of Him as a Father. They know His tender, loving side that wants to care for us and provide for us. Yet, if they are not careful, they can dismiss His power, discipline, and His dislike for sin as the righteous God that we serve. Then there are some people who will acknowledge that God is God and He is also a Father, but it is in a limited way, based on their understanding of earthly fathers. If their earthly father was good then God must be good as well. If their earthly father was abusive, impatient, intimidating, uncaring, moody, or only providing out of necessity and not one who showed much attention or care, then their viewpoint of God as a Father is often directly related to this. This is why Jesus came to reveal Abba and why it is important for us to understand Him today for who He really is and not based on our own experiences or viewpoints.

These two sides of the nature of God can be seen in other places in Scripture as well, where they reveal Him as God *and* Abba. They show His might and power as well as His tender side of mercy that comes with being our heavenly Father. His mercy and justice is seen throughout the Scriptures.

Examples of God and Father

Let's look at a few examples to better understand that He is both God *and* Father. One such example is found in part of a conversation between the prophet Nathan to King David about his son Solomon, who would be next to ascend the throne. It shows us something about the Lord being God and Father. We see that God would act as a Father in righteousness and justice by having to chasten Solomon if he commited iniquity. God said through Nathan,

> *I will be his father, and he shall be My son. If he commit iniquity, I will chasten him with the rod of men, and with the stripes of the children of men: but My mercy shall not depart away from him, as I took it from Saul, whom I put away before thee* (2 Samuel 7:14-15).

This chastening of the Lord is not to be confused with the human concept of harshness or abuse. The correction God brings and wants us to emulate is always in love and righteousness. He does and will chastise those whom He loves! This is why the writer of Hebrews states:

> *And ye have forgotten the exhortation which speaketh unto you as unto children, My son, despise not thou the chastening of the Lord, nor faint when thou art rebuked of Him: for whom the Lord loveth He chasteneth, and scourgeth every son whom He receiveth* (Hebrews 12:5-6).

It is important in our comprehension of how God disciplines His children and in our understanding of Him as our Abba and almighty God, that we don't base it on our own negative experiences with others. Instead, it must be according to what He has revealed of Himself through His Word and His involvement in our lives. God is our Father and His every intention or action is for our benefit and good. We need to be assured that it will always be just and honorable toward us. This is why we need to understand Him both as Abba and our almighty God.

The understanding that He is God and Father doesn't mean to imply that the Father's heart is only one of love, comfort, and forgiveness, while His deity as God is only of judgment, discipline, and correction. A Father is also one who disciplines, corrects, and trains His children. This is the role of a true loving father and failure to do so means they are not acting as a true father.

True biblical love, God's kind of love, confronts, disciplines, and gets righteously angry. This means if there is ever a correction from the Lord, it will always be done properly in the true essence of love. This is because it is just as much His love displayed when we are disciplined, corrected, and chastised by Him as it is when we receive mercy and forgiveness from Him. We can rest in the assurance of His goodness that any discipline or correction from Him in our lives is always done in pure love and with our best interest in mind.

Jesus showed this kind of balanced love in the revealing of His Father. How did He do it? It was by loving the unlovely with compassion and comfort; but He was also righteously angry when He cleansed the temple. He did this with such zeal and righteous anger as He drove the crooked moneychangers right out onto the streets!

Just because God's actions as a Father may appear firm, again, it is always still in love and will bring the needed discipline into our lives. This means we should not be afraid of His love when it brings the necessary changes that we need in our lives. This is because, as our Abba, He will discipline or chastise those whom He loves or we are not His true children. Again, the writer of Hebrews states: *"If ye endure chastening, God dealeth with you as with sons; for what son is he whom the father chasteneth not? But if ye be without chastisement, whereof all are partakers, then are ye bastards, and not sons"* (Heb. 12:7-8).

Proper discipline from Abba will bring true fear of Him as our God. We must always remember that He is love, but He is also a consuming fire through that love. He disciplines those He loves as His children and it must be understood that it is still as much out of His love that He does this. We must never forget that God's love comforts us but can also discipline, correct, and be firm with us if needed. He is a good Father and is there to comfort us in our times of trouble, when things go bad or when we feel down. Yet, because He is an amazing heavenly Father, He will lift us up. How about the times when we need to get up, start over, or feel discouraged? Again, as our Abba, He will be there for us with His comfort but He may also show us His Father's disciplinary side that will discipline and correct us if we need it so we will change. This loving discipline of the Father is not to crush us, condemn us, or make us afraid to approach Him. It is to bring the healthy fear of Him into our hearts, shaping us and developing our character to reflect Him!

It is helpful for us to know Him as both our Abba and our wonderful God. We must accept His loving discipline of us and also bask in His mercy, love, and compassion for us as well. In all things we come to trust Him as our Abba, our heavenly Daddy, who knows best!

In the passage we read earlier in Second Samuel 7:15, when God spoke to King David about his son Solomon through the prophet Nathan, the Father's heart was also revealed by showing that His mercy would not depart from him either: *"But My mercy shall not depart away from him..."* This again is a perfect balance of both God and Father.

Another example can be found when we see how the Lord is both God and Father by our understanding of what He did in the Garden of Eden when Adam and Eve sinned. He drove them out of the Garden as part of the consequences and necessary discipline concerning their sinful actions (see Gen. 3:24). This reveals the righteousness, holiness, and justice of God. The other example we find is in the guarding of the tree of life by the angels. The cherubim guarded the tree of life so that Adam and Eve would not be lost in their sin forever. This is the nature of our heavenly Father to protect us in His mercy and make sure our well-being is taken care of.

Some other examples of God being both our God and Father include:

The two angels on the mercy seat and the throne of God:

There were two angels on either side of the mercy seat that sat atop the Ark of the Covenant (see Exod. 25:19). This was to depict God as the righteous judge of all things on the one side and His Father's heart of mercy on the other. This mercy seat was an earthly representation of the heavenly throne of God, the place where Abba rules as God, the judge over all creation. When the end of all things has come, we will stand before His throne and He will separate the sheep from the goats. The goats will enter eternal punishment, revealing His justice as God, and His sheep will enter into Heaven, revealing His love as our heavenly Daddy. Then we will live with our Father forever in Heaven as His born-again children (see Matt. 25). These are the two characteristics of Abba. But, unfortunately, most only know the judgment side of Him and don't comprehend His mercy.

The two wings of an eagle:

When God delivered the children of Israel from Egypt, He told them that He delivered them and brought them out on eagles' wings (see Exod. 19:4). Again, these two wings represent Abba Father and God being the same person but two distinct roles. One wing represents God as a corporate Father who took careful, compassionate care of the children of Israel, where their shoes and clothes never wore out (see Deut. 8:4). He even provided heavenly food called manna in the wilderness. The other wing represents almighty God, the all-powerful One, who defended His children and showed His might against Pharaoh and the armies of Egypt and the giants of Canaan.

As we have discovered from these examples, He is both God and our Father—and having a good working knowledge of both is vital for our walk with Him. The Lord is always eager in showing us who He is. This is why we need to study the Scriptures and spend time with Him, so He can show Himself to us greater than we have ever known.

The Grand Reveal

God had a great desire for His people to know who He was. He told them to get ready and be prepared to meet Him, for He was going to come down and introduce Himself (see Exod. 19). It was the grand reveal to show Israel who He truly was. He came to reveal that He was both their God and their Father. Yet, again, there was a restriction in that Abba couldn't fully reveal Himself as He desired because the blood of Jesus had not yet redeemed His children and reconciled them to Him. So the only way He could have access to them and they to Him would have to be through Jesus's shed blood on the cross. However, that was still a plan in process and He greatly desired to be with His people, Israel, and for them to know Him at the present.

Due to the fact that His Son, Jesus, had not yet come into the earth, even though He was promised, dating all the way back to what He spoke to Adam, He had to be very wise as not to harm the people in His introduction, because the ultimate sacrifice that would be paid by Jesus had not yet happened. If the people came too close to Him, they would die (see Exod. 19:12). The Lord had to put up boundaries concerning the people so as not to harm them. This, I can only imagine, would be hard for Abba, who wanted nothing more than to be with His people more intimately. Again, even Moses, who acted as Israel's mediator between God and Israel, was limited to friendship. Even the mere gaze upon God's face by Moses in his flesh would be a sure death: *"For,"* God said, *"there shall be no man see Me, and live"* (Exod. 33:20).

It was now time for the Lord to introduce Himself as the people's God and Father. They had waited three days to meet Him. It was the moment they and Abba had been waiting for. The day had finally arrived and God showed up, and as a result there was shaking, lightning, thunder, hail, and fire as His presence came onto the mountain (see Exod. 19:16-18).

He came to reveal Himself as their God and Father, except His grand reveal frightened the people and they ran from His presence instead of to it. They even insisted on Moses going to meet and speak for them because they were greatly afraid (see Exod. 20:18-21)!

The people's reaction to God coming to introduce Himself to Israel is a lot like people today. This is because it isn't so much that people are afraid of His presence, as they are afraid of His power. Their reaction was because His introduction was different and more powerful than they expected! They had a preconceived idea of who God was and how He should manifest Himself to them. And people are still doing the same thing today when it comes to the Lord being both our God and Father.

It isn't often as much the presence of God that people run from or resist, but His power! This is because people often want God on their terms or what makes them comfortable rather than the way God chooses to reveal Himself to us through His Word and by His Spirit. Have you ever noticed that people are usually comfortable with His presence but uncomfortable and resistant to His power? Sometimes, people welcome the "goose pimples" when they feel His presence or they feel comfortable when they sense His peace.

Yet, it is another thing when He chooses to reveal that He is God almighty with great power! He comes and heals the sick, delivers the oppressed from evil spirits, and displays His mighty signs, wonders, and miracles. The result is like with Israel—people often run and will have nothing to do with this. Yet, it is just as much God showing Himself and wanting to be with His people as the tranquil, awesome presence of God that comes when they feel comfortable. It is interesting to see the reaction of people today just like with Moses in his day.

Today, sometimes people can become afraid and either resist Him, mock it, or explain it away as not being their "thing" (see Acts 2:12-13). Sadly, this is why churches are full of people who have never seen the true power of God in demonstration like we read in the Bible or the Book of Acts. And this is why many churches presently, in America especially, have sold out trying to be so relevant toward the culture of the day, yet without any true power of God displayed in their midst. They are afraid that people may run from their churches as they did in the days of Moses. They become more concerned about pleasing people than welcoming and pleasing God. They somehow think that a display of God's power is too much for them to handle.

However, on the day of Pentecost, the Lord waited until He had an audience of people from every nation and tribe before choosing to display His power (see Acts 2:5). He wasn't afraid of an audience or concerned of what people would think! It shouldn't be that people run away from churches where the God of power is present. Instead, they go running to seeker-friendly churches where they seek to please the visitors and people don't make room for God's power to be demonstrated. In many of these type of places of worship, the Lord's power is often not seen in great manifestation.

Sadly, there are few who ever witness a miracle of healing or deliverance right before their eyes in our day and time. But if this culture or the church ever needed anything, it is a healthy understanding of the Lord as both God and Father. Yes, they need to witness His love as Abba, but they also desperately need to experience the power of God. This is especially true when He comes suddenly to heal, to deliver, to save, and to cause people to wonder in amazement at His mighty acts. We must not put God in a box, meaning to restrict Him. This is why He came suddenly in the Book of Acts to fill the people with His Spirit and show His mighty signs, wonders, miracles, and healings!

The Bible says He came "rushing" (see Acts 2:2). In other words, He was in a hurry to be inside man through His Spirit. It was no longer that He couldn't come and show Himself as both God and Father. He could reveal Himself as Abba and as an almighty, powerful God in us, through us, and for us! He does this so He can show His love and power to a generation and a people that desperately need it.

Abba doesn't want to be restricted by men; He wants to now be displayed through and in our lives as God *and* Abba. I think we need to let Him! How about you? This is why we must have a healthy understanding and balance of God and Father in our lives. We must never restrict Him and put God in a box!

Abba in a Box

The Lord never wants to be restricted as our God and Father. However, often today, people, leaders, and churches put Him in a box, restricting Him from moving how He wants to move—with power. God used to be in a literal box—the Ark of the Covenant. He so much wanted to be with His people as their God and Father that He chose to contain His presence to a box. It wasn't just any old box; it was called the Ark of the Covenant that was shaped like a box to contain His presence (see Exod. 25:8, 22). Have you ever heard the phrase "don't put God in a box"? Well, God chose to become God in a box, which would be carried by the priests. Yet He doesn't want to be God in a box today. He wants to be free to manifest Himself powerfully as our God and tenderly as our Abba. He wants to be Daddy in our hearts and carried with us everywhere we go and involved in every facet of our lives.

Why would God choose do this? It was because He wanted to be with His people in such a great and intimate way. It was like we have seen throughout this book that God the Father wanted to be with His children; He wanted to show that He would be their God and Father. This is expressed through the Bible but certainly can be understood since the time of Adam as well. He wanted to be with His creation so badly, to walk with them as He had with Adam, but could not due to sin.

God wanted to be with His people so much that He had worked His plan through the ages, through Abraham, Isaac, and Jacob, and through Moses with Israel. Again, He doesn't want to be shoved into a box, being restricted to a corner and simply forgotten. God wants to be present with us, walking with us as our Abba. He proved this in the Old Testament by choosing men to reveal Himself to. This was even though He would be limited in His ability to truly reveal who He was.

It is amazing how much more He personally wants to reveal Himself to us as Abba with intimate access and relationship with Him. It is so wonderful that we now have full access to Him through Jesus and need to pursue Him with our whole hearts. Let's not put Him in a box any longer or forget about Him, but allow Him in our lives and hearts. It's incredible to think that if He was willing to put His presence in a box just to be with His people, just how much that shows His desire to be with you and me.

He is our God; but better yet, our Abba! I think it is time to put Him in our day-to-day routine and let Him walk with us, talk with us, and be our Abba. I am ready! You can count me in! How about you? Let's go for it and let Abba be revealed in our lives!

Note

1. We will refer to him using his changed name, *Abraham,* in the rest of this chapter as we look at his incredible relationship with Abba.

Chapter Five

Jesus Revealing Abba

*I have revealed You to those whom You gave
Me out of the world* (John 17:6 NIV).

Abba was ready! It was time for His Son to be born into the earth in order to manifest His plan and bring it to completion. Angels were summoned to make this grand announcement of His gift to all mankind. The darkness of the night was the moment chosen to declare through the angels' lips, "Peace on earth, and goodwill toward men" (see Luke 2:14). Shepherds watching their flocks would not fully understand such a grand reveal and declaration from Heaven. The Lamb of God was coming to save all peoples! It was something so intimate and so special; it was not just something but rather someone! God's mystery was being revealed in a very different way than most would expect. Before this announcement would be made, there would be a grand birth and a family selected to bring this plan from a manager, a stable fit for a flock and not an infant. Abba was giving of Himself to be revealed through His Son.

It would be through those mentioned previously that God would choose to bring this about. They would be carefully watched and selected by Him. Who would the Father now choose to be the earthly family entrusted with His Own Son, God in the flesh? It would have to be someone who would be part of the lineage of Abraham to uphold the covenant promises that were made between him and God. They would have to be carefully and strategically selected. They would have to possess some of the traits we saw with Abraham, a true example of an earthly father devoted to God and his own children. They would have to be those who would help to reveal Abba .

Things were at a different level and it was a dark time. There was a desperate need for a true light to come to save all men. What humanity didn't know was that Israel and the earth were about to be brought to a whole new level of just who God is and how He wanted to be revealed as Abba. This would be something He had waited for and the very thing to bring His created sons back to Him through Jesus.

Who now would He choose to best represent Him and His plan? Who would it be? It would be a young woman and a man both chosen by Heaven and carefully watched by Abba to carry out His marvelous plan!

Mary and Joseph would be chosen as the earthly parents entrusted to bring forth the birthing of His Son and to carry on His heavenly plan. If Abba was to rescue His lost family, the created race of man, then He would need the right family to do it through. The time had now come to give His Son to gain back a family of both Jew and Gentile, making up His lost creation from the days of Adam and Eve. The result would be what He had long waited for—the family of God would now be restored, reconciled back to Him.

It was time for this Child to be born and a Son to be given, born of a virgin, and the very government resting upon His shoulders (see Isa. 9). It wasn't just any child or any normal son who was to accomplish this; but His name would be called

Wonderful, Counselor, Mighty God, Everlasting Father, and Prince of Peace. His name would be Jesus! He would be the One who would rescue the lost creation of man and bring them back to Abba through Him!

Abba and Mary

Mary would not expect anything unusual until a voice spoke to her, revealing the plan of Abba. It was the voice of the angel Gabriel sent from the Lord to tell her that God had selected her to carry out His plan and to extend the heavenly family on earth, ultimately bringing them back to Him. What was it about Mary that got Abba's interest, anyway? The Bible tells us that she exemplified qualities of an earthly mother that revealed the heart and nature of God Himself. She would have faith, devotion, love for God, and would believe His word above all else.

Mary lived her life in purity before the Lord. She was a young virgin chosen by Him, believing His word spoken to her, and trusting that what He said would come to pass. Luke tells us that after the angel revealed God's plan to her, *"Mary said, Behold the handmaid of the Lord; be it unto me according to Thy word. And the angel departed from her"* (Luke 1:38). The word she heard from the angel Gabriel, told her not to fall into doubt or unbelief concerning this issue. He would instruct her to not lean on her own understanding by looking to men, but she was to look to God's word and trust it completely.

This is exactly what the Lord wants from us as well. You see, Mary represents what Abba is looking for in us as believers. He wants those who will walk pure, remain faithful to the word of the Lord, and be a person of honor. We can see this trait in Mary regarding staying faithful to what was told her, even though she had opportunities not to. She would remain honorable in her heart and to God's plan.

For example, you can see this about Mary as you look at her life. It was even before the time of our Lord's birth that she believed the word spoken to her by Gabriel. She was seen many times throughout Jesus's earthly ministry, being a part of what He was doing. She followed Him as He carried His cross on the road to Golgotha. She even stood by the wooden cross, as her own Son was dying, bruised, bloodied, beaten, and crucified. I am convinced as she watched her suffering Son, that she even recited in her heart the words prophesied to her by Simeon at the time of Jesus's dedication in the temple, when He was only eight days old: *"And a sword will pierce your own soul too"* (Luke 2:35 NIV).

Jesus, knowing this and being sensitive to how she was feeling, did something so amazing and profound in reaching out to His mother from the cross. It was a beautiful picture of the revealing of Abba through Jesus. It was from the cross that the Lord honored Mary as her firstborn Son. He took the legal responsibility He had as this firstborn son under Jewish tradition to make sure she would be taken care of. He would make sure as a widow that all her needs were being accounted for.

We can further see Abba revealed to us today by Jesus's concern for Mary's well-being in the midst of His pain. In the same way, He cares for our well-being, our pains, and our hurts. In the midst of His own pain and suffering, Jesus was more concerned for the indescribable hurt His mother was feeling and her well-being than He was for His own. This is seen by His entrusting of Mary to John's care while hanging upon the cross.

When Jesus therefore saw His mother, and the disciple standing by, whom He loved, He saith unto His mother, Woman, behold thy son! Then saith He to the disciple,

Behold thy mother! And from that hour that disciple took her unto his own home (John 19:26-27).

How comforting to know that if He cared for her well-being in such a way, that He certainly cares about ours as well. He displayed this by putting Mary's needs before His own. The fact that He was being crucified for us as an innocent man is continued proof of Him putting our needs before His own. Oh, what an awesome Savior we have in Jesus!

We should be comforted and encouraged that as we enter into deeper intimacy with Him as our God, putting His needs above our own, then all other things, like He said, would be added unto us (see Matt. 6:33).

We see Mary again after Jesus arose from the dead in the upper room waiting for the promise of the Father, the infilling of the Spirit. Why? Again, it was because she believed His word spoken to her and she was a person of honor. She was obedient to His word and hungry for His Spirit. We need to be people of honor today, just as she was, and can certainly learn from her life. When it comes to our walk with Abba, we need to believe His word like she did and be honorable to Him. We need to read, study, and meditate on the Scriptures daily as we uphold the righteous standard of honor to our Lord Jesus.

Why honor? It is because honor pleases the Lord. It is what Jesus taught us to do when we pray to our Father who is in Heaven (see Luke 11:2). Honor is powerful and something that is missing today. What is this honor we speak of? It is integrity, honesty, and doing what is right in all situations. Think for a moment about how honor gets the Lord's attention. After being crucified, He gave His body to be buried in a tomb to a man named Joseph of Arimathea, who was an honorable man (see Mark 15:43). Again, He entrusted His own mother to John the beloved because he was the only one that honored Him through His death, standing at the cross while the others forsook Him.

It's not hard to see why Mary was chosen to carry in her womb our blessed Savior and Lord. In the same way, we must honor our Lord as we carry His presence within us. Remember, it is Christ within us, the hope of glory (see Col. 1:27). Mary honored and so must we!

In order for the Lord to complete His plan on this earth, He would need not just Mary but also Joseph to emulate what a true family, with God at the center, looks like. He didn't just need a godly young woman to bring forth a child. He needed a father also. This is why He looked to Joseph and Mary together—He wanted them to represent His plan on earth as the family He chose.

So Abba Father had His eye on this earthly father to be the husband to Mary and the earthly father to Jesus. He looked for a godly man to be that father and that is why He found Joseph!

Abba and Joseph

The mere fact that God would include Joseph reveals Abba's character to us today. It shows us how involved He wants to be as our heavenly Father, but it also points to the vital role that earthly fathers have in each of our lives. When forming a true family according to biblical marriage, it requires the father being involved in conceiving a child with his wife. However, that is not the end of their responsibility or role. They must now be involved in the child-rearing process and help raise the child. Now we understand the case with Jesus being conceived in the womb of Mary by the Holy Ghost:

> *This is how the birth of Jesus the Messiah came about: His mother Mary was pledged to be married to Joseph, but before they came together, she was found to be pregnant through the Holy Spirit* (Matthew 1:18 NIV).

The birth of Jesus obviously had nothing to do with sexual relations between Mary and Joseph. Yet, what it involves is the choosing of Joseph to be the honorable man of Abba's selection. Joseph would fill the needed role of an earthly father in Jesus's upbringing—he had qualities Abba liked.

He had, much like Abraham, certain traits and character qualities that a true father needs to possess. Yet, most of all, he had qualities like Abba. He wasn't just a man chosen but a father, an earthly daddy to Jesus. This choosing of Joseph to care for Abba's Son on earth was greatly considered. God wanted someone who would best represent Him as Abba, a papa, a daddy.

Joseph was chosen because he emulated God and his Daddy's heart and character. Remember when Adam and Eve sinned? Who would stand by them? Who would provide, protect, care, and offer a solution full of love and sacrifice? It would be none other than Abba Father. In the same way, Joseph would have to do these same things, especially in the raising of Jesus from birth. He would have to protect Jesus from King Herod, provide for Him as they relocated to Egypt, and show love to Him even though he was not His biological father.

When looking at the brief mention of Joseph in Scripture, we can conclude that he obviously was sensitive to the shame of another. When his wife became pregnant by someone else, he offered to have a quiet divorce: *"Then Joseph her husband, being a just man, and not willing to make her a public example, was minded to put her away privily"* (Matt. 1:19).

It was also due to him being a just and honorable man. He was going to secretly divorce Mary, so as not to shame her or subject her to the consequences of being with a child out of wedlock. But it wasn't until the angel of the Lord warned him that he refrained from doing so:

But while he thought on these things, behold, the angel of the Lord appeared unto him in a dream, saying, Joseph, thou son of David, fear not to take unto thee Mary thy wife: for that which is conceived in her is of the Holy Ghost (Matthew 1:20).

God likes honor and that is what Joseph had. Honor will always receive Abba's attention, favor, and blessing upon our lives. Not only was it a life of honor as to why Joseph was selected, but also because he was a righteous and just man. This is seen in his actions toward Mary and revealed that he was a kind and sensitive man. As we mentioned when Mary told Joseph she was pregnant, he had every right to feel disgraced. He knew the child was not his own, and Mary's apparent unfaithfulness carried a serious social dishonor in the community. Joseph not only had the right to divorce Mary, but under Jewish law she could be put to death by stoning. Although Joseph's initial reaction was to break off the engagement, the appropriate thing for a righteous man to do was to treat Mary with extreme kindness. He did not want to cause her further shame, so he decided to act quietly. This was not a cover up by sinful deceit, but rather in regards to honor and righteousness so the will of God could be fulfilled in the earth through them.

He could have kicked Mary or baby Jesus to the curb, so to speak, once it was told him that she was pregnant with the Lord. He had a free will and could have chosen to disobey the Lord even after being warned in a dream that this was of God. But he would remain a committed, faithful daddy of a child that He didn't birth. He would care, nurture, raise, provide, protect, love, and cherish this child as his own.

This would reflect Abba's character in that Joseph would adopt God's Own Son in the earthly realm. He would agree to be the earthly daddy who would emulate Abba. Have you heard the saying, "It takes one to know one"? Well, God, being a Daddy, saw this in Joseph! This adoption process would take on the form of what would later become a spiritual adoption in all who would be born again thereafter, where we are spiritually reborn and adopted into sonship through Jesus. This is why the Spirit cries out, "Abba, Father," reconciling the children to their Father and the heavenly Father to His sons and daughters (see Rom. 8:15). And this is exactly the same with Joseph receiving Jesus and adopting Him as his own!

You and I are just as special to God and have been spiritually adopted as His dear children. We are important to Him and must remember something about His character. Please do not presume that those we have read about in this book are more special, important, or loved than you or me. We know God is not a respecter of persons. But there are qualities, traits, and attributes that draw His presence and attention to us like a magnet.

If He chose them, then He will choose us to do great things and carry out His will in the earth. The more we want to be like Him, the more He is drawn to us. There should never be any greater desire and honor from our hearts to Him than to please Him and be like Him. After all, He is our God and Abba. I know I am determined to be one of the first in line for His hand to be upon me to carry out His heart intentions in the earth. This is what He desires.

I am ready to say, "Move out of the way, earth, because there are those who want Abba and His Son, Jesus, more than life itself, and are willing to sacrifice all just like Joseph and Mary." I want Him to know that He can count on me. How about you?

Jesus Came to Reveal Abba

Mary and Joseph carried out Abba's intentions and enjoyed firsthand being close to the Lord. Imagine how it must have been as they held Jesus as a child, hearing His cries, tending to His needs, and the exchange of smiles taking place. Experiencing those tender moments when He would look at them with eyes of love and witnessing His first words! It was exactly what Abba wanted and it would be the perfect picture of a heavenly family reborn. God wanted to be held close to our hearts as seen with Jesus being intimately held close to Mary and Joseph's heart. It wasn't just them that enjoyed those personal touches and times with Him, but it was also God who needed the closeness of man's love as well. This is what He wants from you and from me—He wants that closeness, those personal, intimate times of being together with Him.

In the times leading up to Jesus, many people only understood God as their Creator. They trembled at the thought of Him and were afraid of His power and holiness. It was for this reason that people were afraid to approach God, and why they needed Jesus to reveal His Abba as one of affection and personal love. He was sent to the earth to reveal Him as our heavenly Daddy, and that is exactly what He did. In His prayer to the Father, He said, *"And I have declared unto them Thy name, and will declare it: that the love wherewith Thou hast loved Me may be in them, and I in them"* (John 17:26). What name was Jesus referring to in this verse? It was the name *Father* or *Abba*.

This revealing of Himself as Abba was so special that He wanted it to be His only begotten Son, Jesus, who would have this honor. Have you ever thought why the announcement in the days of creation was, *"In the beginning God created the heaven and the earth"* (Gen. 1:1)? Notice that it didn't mention that in the beginning "Abba" created the heavens and the earth. How about another time when it was God who wanted to make man in His image? Again, it wasn't Abba's name that was mentioned, but rather God's. What is the difference? God didn't mention Himself as Father or Abba even though He was. He wanted that honor to be His Son Jesus's!

God being revealed as Abba wouldn't fully happen until Jesus stepped into the earth so the true revelation of Abba could be understood. This is why, when you read the Old Testament, you will see very few verses that God is referred to as Father. In the Old Testament, the word *father* appears over 540 times. But only a very small amount of those are a reference to God as a Father. Yet, in the New Testament, the word *father* appears 300 times, 256 of which are in reference to God as a Father—the *F* being capitalized in the King James Version.[1]

The reason *Father* appears so many times in the New Testament is because Jesus came to reveal Him! In many of the writings of the prophets in the Old Testament, God had to continually reminded Israel that He was their Father and that they had forgotten Him. By the time Jesus was born, however, the Jews were not seeking Him as He desired, seldom mentioning the word *Father* or allowing it to be spoken from their mouths.

God was limited in being able to truly reveal Himself as a Father, and certainly as Abba, our personal heavenly Daddy, throughout the Old Testament. He could not be revealed as such until Jesus would reveal Him. Before the Lord would be crucified, mankind couldn't fully understand nor have access to their heavenly Father because of sin. They could only have access to Abba through Jesus, both personally and intimately. This is why Jesus told Philip, *"I am the way, the truth, and the life: no man cometh unto the Father, but by Me"* (John 14:6).

Man needed a mediator who went to God on his behalf atoning for sin. Since Jesus has now died and risen again, man has been forgiven of their sins through His shed blood. This means we now have direct access to God as our heavenly Abba. This doesn't require someone else to take our prayers before Him because Jesus paid the price for all sins. He became the mediator between God and men, giving them access to God like Adam had before the fall, in order to walk with God in this intimate fashion.

This is why Jesus came to the people of the earth, revealing Abba and telling them of His love and desire for them to return to Him. Jesus taught the people that it was okay to call God their Father and it was something they should do when they prayed (see Luke 11:2).

It was strange to their ears when He referred to His Father as Abba, His heavenly Daddy. This was especially true among the Pharisees and religious leaders of the day. It angered them, and they accused Him of blasphemy. Jesus was often seen on many occasions having a discourse with them over who God was and if He was truly the Son of this Abba (see John 8).

The reason for this goes back to what we mentioned in the first chapter regarding Jesus and the Pharisees. We will refer to the same article that we previously mentioned by David Alsobrook, called, "Why Did Jesus Call God 'Daddy'?" It sheds even further light as to why the religious rulers hated Jesus revealing Abba, so much so that they crucified Him and accused Him of blasphemy when He said He was the Son of God. Alsobrook writes:

> What angered the religious leaders most about Jesus' annoying habit of calling God "Daddy" was that this unlearned carpenter was not only disrespecting God, He was blaspheming Him! By calling Him "Abba" Jesus was claiming an intimacy with God that only a son could claim. He was claiming Sonship with Deity! This was brought up repeatedly at His trial and eventual crucifixion. It was unthinkable to Jewish leaders living at the time of Jesus that any man could be the Son of God, in the way Jesus was inferring with His repeated use of "Abba". True, all of Israel claimed God as their "Abinu" in

the national collective sense. "Out of Egypt have I called My son" Yahweh had said through the prophets. His "son", they believed was the entire nation, not a particular individual.

None of the rabbis even taught that the long awaited Messiah would be God's Son. They were looking for a King, to be certain, indeed, one that would overthrow Rome, but a messiah of natural conception and birth. Jesus, and as His townsfolk in Nazareth knew, Jesus was not fathered by Joseph. In Mark 6:3 they referred to Him as "Mary's illegitimate son" in the Aramaic text. Only a few selected individuals knew the divine secret of Jesus' conception by the Holy Spirit and virgin birth (see Deut. 23:2). Jesus lived with this undeserved stigma, and still does.[2]

When Jesus came to the earth and began His ministry revealing the Father and declaring that He was His Son, one of the first things He did was reveal His Father's name, Abba. Jesus was sent to reveal Him and that is exactly what He did. It was a part of the Jewish custom that if someone wanted to know who someone belonged to, they would find out by asking who their father was. This is why you often see in Scripture people mentioned as the son of David, the son of Jesse, the son of Jonas, or son of Zebedee, to name but a few.

The identity of a child comes from his or her father. This happens when their father names them. Remember that when John the Baptist was born, his father Zachariah was going to name him after himself according to tradition? But God had a different plan, sending an angel to name the child John and silence Zachariah's lips so he couldn't name him after tradition but rather according to God's purpose (see Luke 2).

This is still the role of earthly fathers today; to give their children identity, affirming them and protecting them, speaking their names as something special and loved by their fathers. It is the same in the Kingdom of God as it is run by the principles of the Father and His sons in the Kingdom. It is governed by the revelation and understanding of fatherhood and our identity comes through God our Father by Christ Jesus! Never forget that Abba speaks your name as special and dear to Him. The moment your name is added to the Lamb's book of life, it is no wonder there is such a rejoicing in Heaven! A lost child of Abba has returned to Him! You are dearly loved by your heavenly Daddy, and He loves to whisper your name. Do you hear it? It is your name upon His heart and lips. You are loved and affirmed, for your name is special to your Father.

This is what Jesus spent His life doing, revealing Abba as His Father. But He would also be the people's Father if they would receive His Son sent to them. He wanted them to experience this close, special relationship that He had with His Son. Jesus told many who listened to Him this very thing: *"All things are delivered unto Me of My Father: and no man knoweth the Son, but the Father; neither knoweth any man the Father, save the Son, and he to whomsoever the Son will reveal Him"* (Matt. 11:27).

In most references, when Jesus spoke about His heavenly Father, it was a reference revealing Abba. This seemed odd for a grown man, but Jesus was a real man's man, you could say. He was a carpenter who was considered more than what a carpenter would be. The people said of Him, *"Is not this the carpenter's son? Is not His mother called Mary? and His brethren, James, and Joses, and Simon, and Judas? And His sisters, are they not all with us? Whence then hath this man all these things?"* (Matt. 13:55-56).

Jesus was more than just a carpenter who just worked exclusively with wood. In fact, the actual Greek word for *carpenter* is *tektón*, which implies a craftsman and a general builder. This means Jesus would have had to be skilled in utilizing the materials He had around Him. This wouldn't be easy because in Nazareth, where He grew up, there was relatively little wood but plenty of limestone. So it would be easy to conclude that Jesus most likely had the muscles of a stonemason as well as the hands of a healer. Yet, in His most desperate time in the Garden of Gethsemane, He was crying out in anguish to His Daddy, like a hurting child. You could imagine His words as He called out to His heavenly Father: *"Abba, Father, all things are possible unto Thee..."* (Mark 14:36).

This is not a sign of a weak man, but one who knew who Abba was, who He was, and why He was sent. Yet, He is in Gethsemane showing affection, emotion, and heart, calling out to His heavenly Daddy in His time of need. Some men today would think that is weak or have been taught it is sissy to show that kind of emotion or vulnerability of heart. Not so with Jesus; He fully understood who Abba was and how much He needed Him. He had an intimate relationship with Him and He was never ashamed to let His heart cry, "Abba!" The same is true for us today when we truly know who Abba is, whether we are male or female. Our hearts will cry out to Him as our heavenly Daddy, saying, "Abba, I need You." It should never be considered weak to call God Abba or show our heart and emotion to Him.

The reason Jesus grew so close to His heavenly Father and could show emotion to Him was due to Him being with Abba before He was sent to the earth, becoming God in the flesh (see 1 Tim. 3:16). Another reason was due in part to the lack of an earthly father that came at some point in His young life. There is reason to believe that Joseph died sometime in Jesus's life between His teenage years and the start of His ministry at the age of 30. The Gospels never mention him beyond the account of Jesus ministering in the temple at the age of 12—he is never mentioned again during His earthly ministry or even at the time while He was on the cross. So we can certainly conclude that Jesus had experienced life without an earthly father at some point.

There are many that can say the same about their own lives today. In fact, fatherlessness is a sad but true tragedy. Do you know there is a large percentage of children who grow up without a father and go to sleep every night without one in the home? This is very hurtful to the child, but obviously also to Abba. Even though this might be the case for some, it doesn't have to hinder us from growing close to Abba as our Father. If Jesus grew close to His heavenly Father in spite of not having Joseph around at a certain part of His life, then we can also. He became so close to Abba that He could say that no one knows the Son except the Father, and no one knows the Father except the Son (see Luke 10:22).

Jesus was secure in knowing and calling God Abba, Papa, and Daddy. So must we today. Whenever He would speak about His Father, calling Him Abba, people would be shocked, even angry with His intimacy toward Him. We must not forget, however, that this was something unknown to those among other religions, including Judaism at the time. No wonder it caught people by surprise when Jesus taught that He knew God intimately as His personal Father.

We need to get a true and healthy picture of who Abba is. But how do we do this? I believe this comes as we understand Jesus's mission—He came to show us His Father, which He did by His own life and the way He walked with Abba. Whatever Jesus was doing, He was revealing Abba to a lost and dying world that desperately needed Him.

A Picture of Abba

Do you want to know what Abba is like? Again, look to Jesus because He was a picture of His heavenly Father while on the earth. One of the ways we can see Abba revealed through Jesus was concerning how He treated the children who approached Him. Mark writes,

> *He took a little child and had him stand among them. Taking him in His arms, He said to them, "Whoever welcomes one of these little children in My name welcomes Me; and whoever welcomes Me does not welcome Me but the One who sent Me"* (Mark 9:36-37 NIV).

He never pushed the children away when His disciples and the religious leaders suggested He should. He always took time out to hold them, put them in His lap, and put His hands on them in order to bless them (see Mark 10:13-16). The children came to Jesus because they were drawn to Abba's love in Him. When they ran to be received and blessed of Him, the Lord didn't stop them. It was to be a beautiful prophetic picture that would show everyone that Abba had sent Jesus to bring all the created sons and daughters back to Him.

What a life lesson for us today. The people wanted Jesus to put His hands upon their children to bless them. Isn't this what we all want? It is to truly have the hand of God upon us to bless us.

Many times in Jesus's ministry we see Him taking time to minister and bless children. Every time He did He was showing us a picture of Abba God. It wasn't hard for Him to relate to the needs of children because He was born into the earth and raised as a child Himself. He always expressed tenderness toward them and a reached out to bless them. You saw Jesus healing children from sickness and disease; He delivered them from evil spirits; He raised them from the dead; and He accepted one young person's lunch to feed the multitudes bread and fish. He took special time to express Abba's love and care for them just as He does for us today.

The fact is that He makes it rain upon the just and unjust (see Matt. 5:45). He cares about the needs of every person, even when they resist Him, hate Him, blame Him, and lie about Him, refusing to have very little to do with Him. If the world only knew of His love and who He truly is, then they would run to Him.

He is the same, yesterday, today, and forever (see Heb. 13:8). When you see how Jesus ministered to people during His time on earth, especially the children, it is still how God is reaching out to His children in our time. He waits for us to come to Him and He will not turn us away. He will hold us close to His heart, laughing with us, smiling, and loving us as His very own!

This is why Jesus said unless we become like a child we couldn't inherit or fully receive the Kingdom of God (see Mark 10:15). This is because in the Kingdom of God, our heavenly Father is there and Jesus sits at His right hand. And the only way to receive His benefits is to come like a child, simply returning to our Abba through Jesus. And how do we do that? It is by receiving Jesus as our personal Savior and Lord, by calling upon Him to be saved from our sins. And once we do, we are then adopted into the heavenly family and become sons and daughters of our Father in Heaven.

Jesus blessing the children and receiving them is not the only picture of Him revealing Abba. There are many examples that can be found throughout the Gospels, in the parables, and in the incredible ministry of Jesus. Let's briefly examine a few of the many examples that help us get a better picture of Jesus revealing Abba!

Revealing Abba Through Actions and Words

The first words out of Jesus's mouth that the Bible records are found when He was 12 years old, speaking in the temple (see Luke 2). He was in the temple talking about things concerning the Scriptures to many people who were years beyond him in age. His parents thought that He was with them as they journeyed back home from their trip to Jerusalem and quickly found He wasn't among them, so they began searching intently for Him. They finally found young Jesus in Jerusalem and thus the first words He spoke to them revealed Abba: "Didn't you know I would be about My Abba's business?" (see Luke 2:49). It was Jesus revealing His Father!

He was saying to them what we need to be reminded of today: we all must direct and commit our lives first and foremost in everything we do to be about our Father's business. We belong to Him and we have given Him rights to be in charge of our words and actions through Jesus. It's what He wants, not what we want; it's His will in everything above our own. If we want Abba to reveal Himself to us, then we must put Him first, making Him a priority in our daily lives. This is the message Jesus was revealing the first time His words were recorded in Scripture as a young boy.

Another picture we see of Jesus revealing Abba was to the devil, before He even started His earthly ministry. He was led into the wilderness by the Holy Spirit to be tempted of the devil. For 40 days the devil tempted Him, both day and night, never ceasing during that time. It was the Garden of Eden all over again. It was once again a child, a son of Abba, being tempted. Yet this time this Son wouldn't fall but would rather reveal Abba to the devil.

How did Jesus do this? He never gave into the devil's temptations and revealed to Satan that He wouldn't bow, serve, or worship him. He would only do this unto God because He belonged to Abba—He was His Son. This has to be the same way you and I have to be concerning the devil's temptations.

We must resist him and submit ourselves to Abba completely, and then that mean ole devil will flee away.

There is another important truth we can apply to our life as we look at what the devil tried to tempt Jesus with. Satan hated the fact that Jesus came to reveal the Father, and even used the very words of sonship to tempt Him. The devil said, "If You are the Son of God, then turn these stones into bread" (see Matt. 4:3). What he was really saying to Jesus was, "If Abba is Your Father, and You are His Son, then provide for Yourself apart from Him. After all, You don't really need Him to provide for You and be Your sustenance, as You have Your own power and ability to do it without Him!" The devil is so sneaky and tries to get us to do things apart from Abba. Yet Jesus replied to him, *"It is written, Man shall not live by bread alone, but by every word that proceedeth out of the mouth of God"* (Matt. 4:4). In other words, "Devil, I can do nothing apart from My Father; I depend upon Him so much that I live by every word He tells Me."

What is important to further understand is that this was not just a mere temptation over bread, but rather a fight for spiritual hunger. The message to us today that we can apply to our lives is this: if we are going to have Abba as our Father, then we must trust Him. We need to rely on Him, be committed to Him, and not live our lives apart from Him. Always remember how the devil tried to change Jesus's spiritual appetite, and he will also try to change ours. This is why after Jesus was in the presence of God fasting, praying, and hungering for Abba, the devil came to try to take His spiritual hunger and focus and put it on natural things. This should send a message to us that our first priority is to seek God and His Kingdom first. We must hunger for God because we want Him in our lives and realize we can do nothing apart from Him. It is realizing that the devil is always out to distract our spiritual hunger and will keep us from it by occupying us with the things of this world. We must stay hungry for Him above all else!

When Jesus came out of the wilderness, after being tempted of the devil, He spent His ministry preaching the Kingdom of Abba, preaching messages that showed the people His heavenly Father. He revealed Abba through preaching, teaching, healing the sick, and casting out evil spirits (see Matt. 4:23-24). All of this helped the people get a picture of who Abba truly is.

The famous Sermon on the Mount was a message by Jesus to reveal His heavenly Daddy (see Matt. 5–7). How is this so, you might ask? He taught them what our attitudes and approach to Abba and life in His Kingdom should be like. He tells us not to be anxious, but to trust our Father from day to day. He reveals the very heart and the responsibility of Abba in our lives as One who carefully watches over us, just like He watches over His creation, even knowing if one sparrow falls to the earth. He shows us how much we mean to God and His great love toward us. This is why He said don't take any thought for our life. In other words, if Abba is our heavenly Daddy, we are His responsibility, so enjoy life with Him and trust that He promised to take care of us. All throughout the Sermon on the Mount, Jesus revealed the traits of Abba as good, and continues to give a picture of life with Him and in His Kingdom. In this great sermon Jesus preached, He further shows how we are to relate to Abba through prayer, encouraging us to find a quiet place to spend with Him.

These are obviously a few examples of Jesus revealing Abba to the people of His day and also to us today. It is to help us get a better picture and understanding of who He is and what He does. When it comes to understanding Abba, especially through looking at the life of Jesus, we not only see the Father's love, forgiveness, and care, but we also see His mighty power to save, forgive, heal, and deliver mankind. So when it comes to understanding Abba revealed in our lives through Jesus, we can't exclude the wonderful power He manifested to show His love for us and hatred toward sin, the devil, sickness, and disease.

This is why it is important to understand why Jesus had this kind of power to help humanity. He had power and authority to heal the sick and deliver the oppressed because of His intimate relationship with Abba. He faced persecution, being ridiculed from the people and culture of His day. This was a result of revealing Abba and demonstrating His power to them. Jesus didn't let it stop Him and we must not let it stop us either! We must remember in this evil culture we live in today that not everyone will love and receive Jesus or Abba. They will ridicule us and try to explain away any divine intervention or power of God by humanizing it as they did with Jesus (see Mark 6:1-6).

We just need to rest in Abba's love and comfort, knowing who we are in Him. Those that walk close to Him will be like Jesus, they will talk with an authority that comes from Heaven and carry His powerful presence to heal the sick, deliver people from the power of the enemy, and reveal Abba wherever they go. They will walk in His power to help mankind. It's because they can't help themselves; they want to reveal Abba as Jesus did!

Show Us Abba

Jesus chose disciples, and specifically had 12 that walked more closely with Him and participated in His ministry to reveal Abba and show His power to those that would need it. They were chosen to show His love, His power, His authority, and His concern for humankind. It is why He chose others to carry out this same mission—to show that Jesus was the true Messiah. He told His disciples to do what He did and that is to preach about Abba's Kingdom and then demonstrate His power. He trained them to do this by walking in love, healing the sick, and delivering the oppressed (see Luke 9:1-2). What they were commissioned by Jesus to do is what we are called to do as well today.

Jesus very carefully chose these 12 men at the start of His ministry, just as Abba chose the different ones we read about throughout this book. His choosing of the 12 was very prophetic of something that revealed Abba to us. This was because they represented the 12 tribes of Israel and the restoration of the sons of Abba through Jesus Christ. It was a picture of the family of God that would be born, the church of the firstborn, just like Israel. The reason for this is because Jacob had 12 sons as a part of his family, and God was showing us by the choosing of 12 in Jesus's ministry, that the plan He had promised to Adam and Eve and Abraham was being fulfilled. He was restoring His family! These 12 would be the foundation on which He would establish it.

One such disciple named Philip asked Jesus something that might have not been mentioned previously or understood by many. He said, "Lord, show us Abba!" This was asked of him after hearing Jesus continuing to reveal Him and talk about Him. What was Philip asking? He was asking Jesus to show them who His Daddy was, "Show us Papa!" Inside every human being is the same longing to see their heavenly Father. The problem is that much of the human race doesn't know this. It is why lives are empty as they search to fill that God-given longing and passion, searching inside of them to be reconnected to their heavenly Daddy. They try to fill it with all kinds of things in search of the emptiness in their heart and lives that only God can fill. They don't understand that Abba is longing to be their heavenly Daddy; He just needs them to want Him and seek to know Him for this to happen.

This is exactly what was in the heart of Philip—He wanted to know Abba intimately.

> *Philip said, "Lord, show us the Father and that will be enough for us."*

Jesus answered: "Don't you know Me, Philip, even after I have been among you such a long time? Anyone who has seen Me has seen the Father. How can you say, 'Show us the Father'? Don't you believe that I am in the Father, and that the Father is in Me? The words I say to you are not just My own. Rather, it is the Father, living in Me, who is doing His work" (John 14:8-10 NIV).

Jesus showed him how to find Abba. In the Lord's response, He said, "If you have seen Me, you have seen My Father!" In other words, "If you have seen Me, you have seen My Daddy. I am just like My heavenly Dad!"

How would Philip know about this kind of personal relationship, especially when Israel had never come to know God as a Father personally, but only corporately? It must have been something he heard or that was explained to him at some point in time. It was the very life that Jesus lived before Philip and the disciples that caused this desire to be produced within him. This needs to be in our life as well. People need to look at us and, by our speech, conduct, and actions, see that there is something different about us. We represent Jesus our Lord and Abba our heavenly Father. It is like the children who came to Jesus— people are drawn to us because of the presence of God inside of us.

It is obvious that Philip heard Jesus addressing God as Abba, thus the reason he asked to know more about Him. He recognized Jesus was revealing something different than what he and Israel had heard or he wouldn't have asked the question in the first place. No one had ever asked this question as far as the Bible records. Whether Philip realized it or not, his heart was starting to cry, "Abba!" He was asking Jesus, "Show us the Father!"

Those must have been words that Abba and Jesus had waited a long time to hear. This is the same thing that they wait to hear from us today and needs to be the cry of every one of our hearts.

"Show us Abba! Reveal Him to us!" Our hearts are crying out, "Abba, Father!"

Notes

1. This was from a Bible search of the term "father" on http://www.biblegateway.com.

2. This article can be found on David Alsobrook's website: http://www.davidalsobrook.com.

Chapter Six

Forsaken?

And about the ninth hour Jesus cried with a loud voice, saying, Eli, Eli, lama sabachthani? that is to say, My God, My God, why hast Thou forsaken Me? (Matthew 27:46).

"Tell us plainly," they sneered. "Are You the Son of God?" He had revealed Abba to them for three and half years. Now they were asking Him what He had already told them and showed them over and over again. The High Priest, the religious council, and the elders all stood with their arms crossed, gathering accusations to try an innocent man of claims that He was the Son of Abba, the Son of God, of royal deity. Yet Jesus stood confident and fully aware that the opening of His mouth would further reveal Abba to them, only causing them to accuse Him still further. No matter what He would say, they still refused to believe or listen to the fact that He truly was the Son of God. He knew that He was sent as Abba's plan to be the true and final Lamb that would be led to the slaughter of beating, whipping, punching, and a horrible crucifixion that awaited Him.

Any word and answer He gave would only, in their minds and through their actions, incriminate Him more. Yet, this only begotten Son of Abba would look deep into their eyes and respond to their question, "Yes, I am" (see Matt. 26:64).

Outraged at His reply, they spit on Him, raising their fists to strike Him on the mouth and beat Him, hitting Him in His face. How could He make such a claim? He showed them, taught them, and revealed who Abba was throughout His entire life. He instructed them about how He was the Son of God and why He was sent to the earth. They wouldn't be convinced—much like this sinful world has refused to believe today. The religious leaders had enough of His statement of being the Son of God and now they needed a reason to put Him to death. With more false accusations against Him, they formulated a reason to crucify Him and charge Him with a crime.

What was His crime? Helping hurting humanity with a supernatural power and love that He claimed came from His heavenly Daddy? These leaders hated this man Jesus and His claims of deity, calling Himself the Son of God and using the name Abba, which is only fit for toddlers. "Blasphemy!" they screamed. "Let's kill Him!"

Trial of Two Sons

They would now deliver the Son of God over to be tried by the governor named Pontius Pilate. Jesus would once again be found having to defend that fact that He was God's only begotten Son. Why couldn't they believe Him? Why was it so hard to see that His claims and actions were true? No one ever born into the earth had truly shown the world Abba like this man; nor had anyone had the evidence, the power, or the teaching of truth to back up His every word than Jesus. However, their hearts would be hardened as some are today despite the evidence, no matter what has been done and provided to them of God's love and forgiveness. They still refuse to believe and will continue to question Him in the foolishness of their hearts, even when enough proof has been shown that He is the Son of God; He is Jesus, crucified, dead, and buried, and risen again; and is now Savior and Lord of all.

The same religious hierarchy stood to further accuse Him of blasphemy and watch Pilate question Him: "Are You really the Son of God; tell me plainly?" Furthermore, "Are You the King of the Jews?" Jesus, not answering much of what was asked of Him prior, would on this question stare intensely back at him with His response, "I am." That answer was enough to send Pilate thinking with trepidation of just who this man was before him and what he would do concerning the accusations against Him.

This is because he was facing his own fears that all of us face: fear of his reputation, fear of shame, humiliation, and a fear for his life and job. This would cause him to have to choose between his own fears and the truth presented before him, all in the presence of the Son of God who stood quietly watching as Pilate struggled.

Pilate sent Jesus to be beaten and whipped by his soldiers; they twisted together a crown of thorns and forced it upon His head. They clothed Him in a purple robe, striking Him in the face and mocking Him, saying, "Hail, King of the Jews!" What they didn't know of their dishonorable act was, just as the coats of skin were put upon Adam and Eve, Jesus would wear this garment to signify Him paying the price of all the sins of humanity, thus fulfilling Abba's plan.

"Do You not know I have power to crucify You?" Pilate asked Jesus after having the Lord scourged, as if to imply he was in control and more powerful than Him who claimed to be Abba's Son. Looking straight at Pilate through His bruised and bloodied eyes reminded Him of just who was in authority, "You have no power unless it had been given to you from My Abba, My heavenly Daddy." This would send shivers down Pilate's spine and echo throughout all of hell. He would wash his hands in fear of responsibility and now let the people decide. In the arrogance of protecting his own reputation, he didn't want the blood of this man, Jesus, upon his hands.

It was a custom once a year for Pilate to release one prisoner and the other to be crucified. Who would the people choose to be crucified and who would be freed though they were guilty of their crime? Two men would stand before God, before Pilate, and the people. One would be Jesus, the only begotten Son of Abba, though innocent of all wrongdoing, would be charged as guilty. The other a man, Barabbas, was a prisoner, a thief, a murderer, and guilty of his crimes. But it was him who would be freed that day.

Pilate summoned the people, "Who do you want me to release for you? Jesus who is called the Christ or Barabbas?" And they would shout out loudly as if all of hell were screaming through their lips, "Crucify Jesus! We want Barabbas." What they failed to realize, and what the devil himself failed to understand, was the prophetic significance of what was happening. It was Abba's plan being revealed from the very days He spoke it to Adam and Eve. Had the hordes of hell known this they wouldn't have crucified the Lord of glory (see 1 Cor. 2:8)! There was something very powerful happening in these two that were standing trial. What is even more profound and how it relates to us is a common parallel that is found in the meaning of their names and identity!

Even though Jesus is the only begotten Son of God, there was something prophetically significant about Barabbas and his name relating to being a son of Abba. The word *Bar* means "son," and *abba*, as we know, means "father." So Barabbas's name literally means "Son of Abba."[1] So we can see how prophetically significant these two standing on trial were—both sons of Abba.

It was two sons of the Father standing on trial that day! This affects us today by the mere fact that Barabbas's name prophetically represents all of us born into the earth as the "lost created sons of our heavenly Father." We are also like him in that we are guilty of our sins and all have the sinful nature of Adam in us. We needed Jesus to offer His life innocently and willingly by paying the price for us through the cross, setting us free. We, like Barabbas, should have been the ones that were punished for our sins rather than Jesus being crucified that day.

Historians and Bible scholars have suggested that Barabbas's first name was also Jesus. The name *Jesus* in the Hebrew means, "the Lord is salvation." So his full name would have been Jesus Barabbas, giving more prophetic truth to the meaning of his name as being a "son of Abba" or "son of a human father that needs the Lord's salvation"! This is amazing as we see God's plan concerning us. We have two sons of Abba standing on trial: one divine Son, innocent yet paying the price for all sin; the other is Barabbas, the created son of Abba who was truly guilty of his crimes and represents all mankind set free through Jesus Christ.

Throughout Scripture God continues to reveal His plan of sending Jesus to reveal Abba. There are some other examples that prophetically show Abba's plan and these two "sons of Abba" that relate to us today:

Cain and Abel (see Gen. 4):

Cain and Abel further show Abba's plan and how it relates to Jesus, Barabbas, and mankind. It is another prophetic example of Jesus being murdered innocently by His brethren like Abel was. Cain, like Barabbas, was also sent into the wilderness, guilty of his sin. In this story with Cain and Abel, we find that Abba is faced with a created son found guilty of a crime committed. Cain murdered his innocent brother, Abel, and was sent away to Nod in the wilderness. This is interesting in the way it further reveals Jesus and Barabbas: one son was considered righteous, pleasing God, named Abel, who brought the firstfruits of his flocks and was accepted by God just like Jesus would be the final offering, pleasing and acceptable unto God. Yet, Cain represents Barabbas, a murderer also, guilty of his crime and sin. And he was sent away with the punishment of sin upon his life.

The two birds (see Lev. 14:1-7):

There were two birds that were used in the cleansing of the leper, which applies to mankind in their sinful nature and their need to be cleansed from their sins through Jesus. One bird was killed in an earthen vessel over running water and the second bird was dipped in its blood and then set free. These two birds have a dual meaning.

First, they prophetically represent the crucifixion and resurrection. This first bird is slain in an earthen vessel, this a foreshadow of Jesus coming to the earth to die as a man. The other bird was set free as to show that He would be resurrected after being crucified. This is why there had to be blood upon this second bird, because without the shedding of the blood of Jesus there would be no forgiveness of sin or resurrection.

The second meaning of these two birds prophetically speaks of the two sons of Abba we discussed earlier. The first bird represents Jesus dying by crucifixion for us and shedding His blood. The second bird represents Barabbas and all mankind that was set free after the blood of the first bird was applied to it. This is amazing how it reveals Abba's plan of sending Jesus to die and His blood put upon us to forgive us from our sins even though we were guilty!

The two goats (see Lev. 16):

Another example revealing Abba's plan and the two sons of the father are seen with two goats in Leviticus 16. The priest would take two goats and present them both before the Lord. The one goat would be killed and offered as a sin offering just like Jesus was. The second goat would be let go in the wilderness, becoming free, called a "scapegoat" just like Barabbas. It is important to remember the word "scapegoat" today means something entirely opposite from what it meant at the writing of our King James Bible. The word *scapegoat*, in modern terms, means to take the blame for others. Yet, in the example here in Leviticus, the goat would actually carry the sins of the people into the wilderness. Remember Barabbas is a type of mankind who is guilty with sin but had his charges dropped, set free through Jesus's death and resurrection.

Fallen Man, the Suffering Savior, and Abba's Love

"Crucify Him, crucify Him," the crowd shouted as Jesus was led away to face death by crucifixion while Barabbas was set free. Jesus is despised and rejected by those He was sent to. He would walk with a wooden cross upon His tired, beaten body. He would remind Himself that He was doing this for us, taking upon Him the sins of all humanity. He is stricken, smitten of God, and afflicted, an innocent man about to be crucified. His appearance is marred beyond recognition to the point where some looking on would hide their faces from Him. The soldiers had scourged Him to the point of death and exhaustion (see Isa. 53).

Jesus has gone without sleep and has had nothing at all to eat or drink since the Passover meal the night before. He is famished, thirsty, and His body is swollen from the deep wounds and bruising from His beatings. He is carrying His cross through the crowds of those that hate Him and those that love Him. Jesus is hearing them laughing, seeing them mocking, feeling some spitting upon Him, and watching others cry as they reach out to Him.

He doesn't complain, defend Himself, or retaliate. With every snicker from the crowd that followed Him and the bullying of the Roman soldiers, He never quit—He just kept pushing forward as His knees buckled, His shoulders gave out, and His back barely able to support what is demanded of Him. As He presses forward, His eyes pierce the very hearts and souls of His onlookers. He sees you, me, and all of humanity. Not once does He harden His heart or desire vengeance, but simply pushes forward.

Multitudes witness Him carrying His cross as His legs are becoming weak underneath the weight of it all. He is alone? Where is Abba while all this is taking place? Where are those that Jesus ministered to: the lepers, deaf, blind, and diseased that were made well by Him? Where was someone—anyone?— from the multitudes He fed to help Him carry the weight of this cross? There is no one to help, to lighten this weight, and ease His pain. The soldiers continue to prod Him, beat Him, pushing Him forward, trying to get Him to walk faster as He carries His cross. The Lord is exhausted but continues His journey on this road to the place called Golgotha to be crucified.

Even though it may not appear like it, Abba was with Jesus during this time. This is because God always had a plan to help us in our journey when we feel like the world's problems are on our shoulders. He will not leave us or forsake us. This is what we will see with Jesus concerning Abba. How do we know?

Because when something happens along this road, He wouldn't leave Jesus's side but provided someone to help carry His cross.

This Son of Abba stumbles as the wooden beam hits the ground, sending a loud thunder throughout eternity, a sound of love and forgiveness that lasts forever. The Roman soldiers, in their pious anger, grab for someone to help carry this innocent man's cross. The soldiers force a passerby, a man named Simon of Cyrene, to carry the cross for Jesus: *"And as they led Him away, they laid hold upon one Simon, a Cyrenian, coming out of the country, and on him they laid the cross, that he might bear it after Jesus"* (Luke 23:26).

From this we can conclude that Jesus had become so weak that it had become impossible for Him to continue to carry the cross any farther. He therefore must have stumbled and fallen at different times. But Abba would use this man along the journey, a man named Simon of Cyrene, to help Jesus bear the weight of the cross. This is after He is stumbling, falling, and being pushed forward to carry His cross. We must remember that the sheer weight of this cross is one of great challenge, especially due to the prior events at the whipping post as chunks of flesh and muscle were torn from Jesus's bloodied back.

It was by them choosing Simon of Cyrene to help Jesus that Abba was sending a message to everyone there, and everyone who would hear about it thereafter. Simon would carry the cross put upon Jesus's back to symbolize our need to pick up our cross daily and follow the Lord (see Luke 9:23). It also shows the condition of all mankind who are the lost children of God and who can't bear their sins alone. Just as Simon would literally grab the cross of Jesus, we need to grab a hold of what Jesus made available through the cross by faith. It shows that we are all in need of a Savior, who is Jesus. We need Him to carry the cross for us and pay the price for our sins so that, in return, we can give our lives to serve Him like Simon did.

Abba was showing a prophetic truth to us and to those that were witnessing this horrible, inhumane treatment of this man, Jesus; not an ordinary man, but now a wounded warrior who healed the sick, delivered the oppressed, loved the unlovely, and was now paying the ultimate price for something He didn't do. This all happened in the name of love—He was fulfilling Abba's plan to restore man back to Himself. The mere fact that Jesus had someone help Him in this horrific journey on this road reveals Abba's mercy and that He would not forsake or leave His Son alone in difficult times.

This is important for us to understand about God because He wants us to know that there is always someone in our path that He will send to help us through difficult times. But most importantly, that someone is Abba Himself. This is to show us today that no matter our journey in life, we don't have to be without hope and carry the weight of our burdens and problems alone. We can have confidence that Abba will be with us and will provide everything we need, even specific people, like Simon was with Jesus. He will bring them along our path to help us; He will give us a hand and pick us up when we fall. You don't have to feel forsaken because you are not alone; He will never leave you or forsake you.

This is why Simon of Cyrene was chosen to help the Lord along His journey. It is to show us that God is always with us in our journey through life. Think about it for a moment. In the midst of a crowd that was pushing, shoving, and yelling, Abba would have the soldiers grab this man Simon, to show that our heavenly Daddy is concerned for our journey in life and the things we face; and He is also concerned for our future.

We learn some very valuable truths when understanding Barabbas as we mentioned before and now Simon of Cyrene. We come to understand that every person is a type of Barabbas, guilty of sins but set free because Jesus paid the price for us. In addition, we are all like Simon of Cyrene in that we are not to be onlookers, but one who grabs hold of the love and forgiveness Jesus provides in the cross and become a true follower of Him.

Abba Promised Not to Leave

Abba is a faithful God and Father. He will not leave us alone or forsake us. We will see this amazing attribute of our heavenly Daddy as we continue to see the events leading to His death on the cross. Did Abba leave His Son? Did He forsake Him?

Deserted by His close followers, who would now stand by Jesus as He faces a horrific crucifixion? If we are to even begin to comprehend what our wonderful Savior suffered on our behalf, then it is important to understand the cruelty of crucifixion. It was so horrible that no Roman citizen, regardless of the crime they committed, would be sentenced to death by this means. The Jewish historian Josephus called it "the most wretched of deaths" and the Roman statesman Cicero called crucifixion "the cruelest and disgusting penalty." Those who understood this inhumane act would fully comprehend the words of Scripture: *"And when they had crucified Him…"* (Mark 15:24). They describe the sure humiliation of being stripped naked and shamed before all to see. These words are few but describe loud and clear the agony and pain Jesus would suffer.

Arriving now at Golgotha, the place where Jesus would be crucified, the soldiers fastened Him to the cross, pounding nails through His hands and feet. He watched as they are being driven through His wrists. With every sound from the hammer hitting the nails, He hears the sound of human heartbeats encouraging Him of the reason He is willingly laying down His life. Gasping for air and feeling the excruciating pain as it pierces His body, He continues to love and forgive as He feels each painful vibration throughout His body with every strike of the hammer.

He is lifted high into the air upon this wooden cross, hanging in the balance between the earth and Abba's throne in Heaven. The angels, who love Jesus and have worshipped Him since their creation, legions of them too numerous to count, stand and watch but do not come to His aid. They don't fully comprehend this marvelous plan of Abba. The Father Himself, who has declared Jesus to be the Son whom He loves and in whom He is well pleased, is also watching. His eye is always on the sparrow, knowing when one falls to the ground. And in the same way, His eye is always on His Lamb, His very Son. Abba is watching every moment of this horrible treatment but does not intervene. In the midst of His unfailing love for His Son, He can't help Him because, if He does, then His plan would be over and mankind would be lost in their sinful nature forever!

His lack of intervention doesn't mean that Jesus was alone, abandoned, or even forsaken by Abba. His heavenly Daddy was there with Him. This is especially the case, since Jesus cried out for Him in the Garden prior to the crucifixion, saying, "Abba, Father" (see Mark 14:36). For Jesus's entire life God would stay true to His Son, staying at His side through every moment of His suffering, including the horrible crucifixion.

God is faithful to His people and He will not leave us or forsake us (see Heb. 13:5). The Lord spoke something to me one day that changed my life and my understanding of Him as Abba.

I had faced various challenges, feeling like some of the attacks that I was facing were more than I could handle. It was one blow and attack after another. It is in those moments that you have to remind yourself that God is faithful and He will help you. I was praying and not sensing much of the Lord's intervention in my life during this time. I was crying out to God when He spoke something that literally shook me. He said, "I will never leave you or forsake you, Hank. I am your Abba Father. I revealed Myself to Israel corporately as their Father and to Moses as a friend. It wasn't until Jesus came that I revealed Myself even more as Abba. I am your heavenly Father and I will not leave you. I am here to help you and will not forsake you. It may not seem like it, but I didn't forsake you and neither did I forsake My Son!"

Those words forever changed me! I heard them so strongly and was completely overcome with what I heard. I pulled a blanket over my head, shaking in His presence. He spoke a few of those words again, "I will not forsake you, and neither did I forsake My Son!" *What?* I thought, as I was shocked by what I heard. "You didn't forsake Your Son?" I asked. Those words would surprise me but also comfort me as I realized I wasn't abandoned or forsaken in my predicament. My heavenly Daddy was there for me as He would be for His Son, Jesus. He promised He would not leave or forsake us, just as He did not forsake His Son, Jesus.

I immediately began to search the Scriptures for what I heard because it seemed different than what I had believed. I had always heard that Abba couldn't look at Jesus as He was dying on the cross, paying for the sins of all mankind, so He had to look away, forsaking Him for just a brief second. When this happened, Jesus cried out from the cross, "My God, My God, why have You forsaken Me?" This is what I had always heard and been taught. Was it because Abba looked away, forsaking Him, or was there another reason for Jesus to cry out this way?

I wanted to look further into this statement Jesus made from the cross and what I believed the Lord had shown me. I began to search the Scriptures and consulted with other well-respected ministries for their input. What I realized was this: Abba didn't forsake His Son and had promised to be with Him at every moment. Jesus had a confidence that His heavenly Daddy would not leave His side. We know this because of what Jesus said regarding His Father being at His side and intervening if He wanted Him to: *"Do you think I cannot call on My Father and He will at once put at My disposal more than twelve legions of angels?"* (Matt. 26:53 NIV).

A Sign

Jesus and His heavenly Daddy were quite close and He counted on God to be there for Him. This would include His crucifixion and the events leading up to it. He was so confident that His Father would not leave Him that He even told this to the Pharisees and His disciples prior to His death on the cross. He revealed to them a sign so they would know that He was indeed the Son of God and His Abba would not leave His side.

He knew the Pharisees would be standing by His cross ridiculing Him, insulting Him, and doubting who He was. They would shake their heads in disbelief and in disgust, thinking His Father had left Him. This is why they would say, "You saved others, now save Yourself" (see Matt. 27:42). Jesus knew they would believe that His Father forsook Him, making Him out to be a liar and their false accusations about Him true. He knew His suffering on the cross would cause them to believe it was His Father forsaking Him and would only build their case against Him.

Yet Jesus gave them a clue that He would not be forsaken of His heavenly Daddy when they saw Him suffering on the cross. He gave them something to remember when this event took place, to show that His Father had not forsaken Him and that He indeed was the Son of God. He told them about this all-important sign to look for:

> *But they still didn't understand that He was talking about His Father.*
>
> *So Jesus said, "When you have lifted up the Son of Man on the cross, then you will understand that I Am He. I do nothing on My own but say only what the Father taught Me. And the One who sent Me is with Me—He has not deserted Me. For I always do what pleases Him." Then many who heard Him say these things believed in Him* (John 8:27-29 NLT).

Jesus was telling them that they would doubt who He was and not believe that His God is His heavenly Daddy. Yet He gave them a sign that reveals who He is and that His Father was still with Him. He told them, "When you lift Me up to crucify Me, I will not be alone! I will not be deserted by Him!" He was telling them, "You think I have lied and blasphemed, but you will see that the Father hasn't left Me." Jesus could say this confidently because He already knew the outcome of what would happen and that His Father would not leave Him.

It is why He could say that He always does what pleases Abba, including what He would speak (see John 8:29). So to think that Jesus was calling out to God on the cross because He was forsaken would not be pleasing to God. It would actually be contrary to what Jesus said would happen between Him and His Father. Remember, He told them that He always does what pleases His Father and that His heavenly Daddy would be with Him. So, to imply that He questioned His Abba as to why He forsook Him would mean that Jesus became doubtful, not believing that His Father would be with Him. To knowingly do this would make Him guilty of lying and mistrusting His Father, which He didn't do.

However, Jesus told them that Abba, who sent Him, is with Him. His Father was at His side! It is important that He does what pleases His Father regarding His death, because Jesus was the pleasing sacrifice to God. He was the sacrifice that was inspected and offered to God as the final Lamb to pay for all the sins of mankind. Once the sacrifice was considered accepted by God, especially the lamb that was killed once a year for all the sins of Israel, then it would be finished and there wouldn't need to be another sacrifice. If God would look away, then that would mean the offering wasn't pleasing and acceptable to Him, thus not being accounted as a worthy sacrifice. This is why it was established beforehand by the priest to inspect the lamb to make sure it was without blemish and could be offered for the sins of the people. Once it was considered acceptable, it was then offered and God would receive it without looking away.

In the same way, Jesus was innocent but was inspected by Herod, Pontius Pilate, the High Priest, and the religious council to be crucified. We know that He was the accepted pleasing sacrifice by Abba, meaning the Father would not need to look away as He hung on the cross. Jesus was killed and shed His blood for the sins of the people. He wasn't rejected or forsaken by God. Just like the sacrificial lambs that were inspected by the priests to be blameless and offered for sacrifice, God wouldn't look away but receive the sacrifice with pleasure. This is what He did with Jesus being the Lamb of God who takes away the sins of the world—He wouldn't look away or forsake Him.

Jesus Became the Offering for Sin

You might be saying, "Yes, but didn't Jesus become sin and that's why He was forsaken and God looked away for a moment?" The Bible says that Jesus is the Lamb of God who was without spot or blemish, as we mentioned earlier (see 1 Pet. 1:19). He was our high priest, yet without sin, never committing sin and neither was there any guile in His mouth (see Heb. 4:15; 1 Pet. 2:22). He was sinless and perfect when He walked this earth. On the cross, He suffered as the offering of sin and not sin itself. What is the difference? If He had become sin, then that would make Him guilty of sin, making Him a sinner. However, if He was the offering for sin, He is guilty of those sins of others by taking the punishment and the penalty of it upon Himself. This means He then became a sin offering and not sin itself, or guilty of it in the sense of a sinner. The reason many feel that the Father forsook Jesus is because it is often thought that Jesus, even though being the perfect spotless Lamb, became sin. He would no more become literal sin than the Father literally forsook Him.

Paul wrote, *"For God made Christ, who never sinned, to be the offering for our sin, so that we could be made right with God through Christ"* (2 Cor. 5:21 NLT). Paul is quoting and alluding to the words in Isaiah 53, where it says that Jesus would become an "offering for sin": *"Yet it pleased the Lord to bruise Him; He hath put Him to grief: when Thou shalt make His soul an offering for sin"* (Isa. 53:10). Understanding this verse in Isaiah helps us to understand Paul's mentioning of it in Corinthians. This is what Paul is also implying in his writing by quoting this passage from Isaiah, that Jesus's death is that of an offering for sin rather than Him actually becoming sin. It is important that Isaiah prophesies that Jesus would be the "offering for sin" and not become sin itself.

Again, as we have mentioned, if you are a sin offering, you are not guilty of the sin itself, even though you are guilty by association, meaning you didn't commit the crime but are taking the responsibility and punishment for it. This is why Jesus wasn't a sinner and didn't become sin, but rather He was punished as a sinner and accused of being one. Furthermore, this is why the sins of all the people were laid upon Him, becoming a sin offering for all of mankind: *"Who gave Himself for our sins, that He might deliver us from this present evil world, according to the will of God and our Father"* (Gal. 1:4).

We know this from the goats and lambs mentioned earlier, and how they would be sacrificed as an offering for sin. When they were killed on the Day of Atonement as a sin offering, it didn't mean they were full of sin or had become sin itself (see Lev. 16). Neither did Jesus, as the perfect Lamb, actually become sin but rather was the payment offered as the full, complete, and ultimate offering for sin. Just as the goat or lamb was a substitute for the people's sin, so would Jesus be the substitute for the people's sin even though He had no sin—He would become the sin offering.

He Is With Me

This helps us to understand why the Father then would not have to look away or forsake His Son. This is, again, why Jesus told the people, *"The One who sent Me is with Me; He has not left Me alone, for I always do what pleases Him"* (John 8:29 NIV). It is important to note what Jesus meant when He said My Father *"is with Me"* and "has not deserted Me." This is because *"is with Me"* is in the present tense Greek, which indicates a continued action and not just implying that Abba is with Him only at that moment. The verb *is* (*eimi*) is a present, active, indicative verb. This means, because it is in the present tense, it is then a continuous action in present time and following. So when Jesus said, "He that sent Me is with Me," He is showing the continual association that would take place between Him and His Father and not just at that present time.

The Amplified Version translates this same verse as saying the Father was ever with Him: "And He Who sent Me is ever with Me; My Father has not left Me alone, for I always do what pleases Him" (John 8:29 AMP).

It means that Jesus, as He walks through the events of His death and resurrection, will never be separated from God because the phrase refers to a continued action. The understanding in the Greek would be that the "One who sent Me is with Me and will continue to be with Me." Jesus is so assured that His heavenly Father will be with Him that He speaks of it to imply presently, will be, and forever! It then would not make sense for Him to declare that God forsook Him on the cross! This is why we are going to carefully examine what Jesus was saying in His statement from the cross, "My God, My God, why have You forsaken Me?"

It is even further evident that Abba would stay at Jesus's side by the phrase: He *"has not left Me."* This phrase is in the aorist tense Greek. The verb, *aphiemi*, translated as "left," is an aorist, active, indicative verb. What this means is that the phrase *"has not left Me"* indicates something that has happened or is happening and the effects of it will continue to take place. In other words, it is not just a current or past event, but Abba will continue to be with Jesus, not forsaking Him or leaving Him alone. And this would include the entire time of His crucifixion!

It is important to understand that when we seek to understand Jesus's question on the cross. If He knew His Father would never leave Him, then there would be no need to think His Father would ever forsake Him. He wouldn't even have to ask the question. So there must be something else we need to consider from His cry on the cross. Was He feeling forsaken? Was He really forsaken or was He making a statement to reveal something else?

When Jesus is telling them that His Father is always with Him, it is showing them the intimate, unbreakable relationship between Him and His heavenly Daddy. He has never been left alone in the past, currently, or in the future. So Jesus could speak confidently about His Father being with Him, especially in the context of the crucifixion. It would be a sign to those that would question Him and not believe at the foot of His cross.

Jesus further revealed that Abba would not leave His side as He spoke to His disciples. He would mention a difference between them and His heavenly Daddy. He would tell them that they would all leave Him, scattering for their own lives, and would be overcome with fear. But Abba would be different! He wouldn't leave His side during the events of the crucifixion like they would. His Father would not leave His side or forsake Him. He told His disciples before the crucifixion: *"Behold, the hour cometh, yea, is now come, that ye shall be scattered, every man to his own, and shall leave Me alone: and yet I am not alone, because the Father is with Me"* (John 16:32).

Jesus is telling His disciples of what is about to transpire concerning His death. He reveals that they will all leave His side but His heavenly Daddy will be with Him through it all. We know this from these phrases *"I am not alone"* and My *"Father is with Me."* This again, is in the present tense Greek, meaning "He has been, is currently, and will always be with Me!" This is the comfort that Jesus had while the disciples would leave, deny, and forsake Him. He wouldn't be alone because Abba would still be with Him. Jesus was showing us that even though it may look like He is forsaken with the inhumane things He would face, it wouldn't be any different from the way it had always been. Abba would not depart from Him but would always be with Him.

So if Jesus told the Jews and His own disciples that the Father would not leave His side, then what was He saying when He asked, "My God, My God, why have You forsaken Me?"

Was Jesus Forsaken?

The sky became dark as the Son of God was bleeding upon the cross, the very doorway that would be open to all mankind who would receive His and Abba's plan. He is barely able to breathe. Lifting Himself up to take in the last few breaths He will ever take as a man sent to this earth, He has calls upon Abba, saying, "Father, forgive them. They know not what they do." His words are now harder to speak with swollen lips and bruised cheeks. He pulls Himself up as strength is leaving His arms as they hang open wide as if to say, "My arms are open wide; come all who are heavy laden and I will give you rest. Come, all who are guilt ridden with sin, I will forgive you and give you peace!"

He is weak and in constant pain as every nerve in His body responds to His suffering. He is not even recognizable to those who stood by as they shake their heads in disgust at Him and His appearance. He is hungry, thirsty, and not able to breathe, let alone speak. Yet, the Son of God would find the strength and the joy set before Him to endure the cross and utter something from His lips that caused those who stood by to suddenly stop and listen: "Eloi, Eloi, lama sabachthani?" Which is to be interpreted, "My God, My God, why have You forsaken Me?" (see Matt. 27:46).

Was Jesus feeling forsaken? Is this an actual question addressed to the Father? Is He actually being forsaken here when He utters these words? What is happening to Jesus? Was He asking why? Or was this a form of intercession for humanity? In all His teachings, references to God, and even in the way He taught His disciples to pray, He always addressed God by calling Him Abba or Father. So why is He now calling Him God and not Abba? In the seven sayings of Jesus recorded from the cross, He addresses God as His Father twice, yet why now is He saying "God" instead of the more intimate term of Abba?

The mere fact that Jesus is making this statement as to call out to God reveals our human need for Him in our lives. It is only by calling out to Him as our God that He then can become our personal Abba. Once we do, our hearts can cry, "Abba!" Here, Jesus, by speaking this from the cross, is also quoting a question every human asks at some point in his or her life. It is the question of why. We must understand that when He was speaking this, it is also a form of intercession for humankind who is asking God the same question.

Why did this happen? Why did my father leave me when I was young? Why am I hurting and in pain? Why do I feel forsaken? You know the questions we ask. Jesus was showing us by this statement that through His death and resurrection to follow that He is the answer to every man's questions of why. He was revealing that we no longer have to question God as to why, because He was dying on our behalf to give man the answers we need that God will not forsake us in this life.

This is why Jesus was making the statement of why, quoting Psalm 22: *"My God, my God, why hast Thou forsaken me? why art Thou so far from helping me, and from the words of my roaring?"* (Ps. 22:1). This is how King David felt when he wrote this psalm and often how we feel today. We can sometimes feel abandoned, forsaken, and even think that God is not listening or helping us. But Jesus quotes this passage of why so we don't have to. It isn't a question He is asking of the Father as much as it is a question mankind asks in this life. It was to also give all mankind hope that His Father is with Him and will be with us also! This is why we discover this isn't Jesus questioning God, but answering a question by quoting a question from this psalm.

Just because Jesus is asking a question doesn't mean that it is an indication of how He personally feels at the time, or that His Father is forsaking Him. Remember, as we mentioned before, Jesus said that He knew Abba would not leave Him and would always be with Him, and instructed to tell others of this very thing.

So it would not make sense to think that Jesus doesn't know what is happening to Him and questioning His Father. Of course, Jesus knows the answer to what is happening and He wouldn't need to question His Father by calling Him God. He is not forgetting what is taking place or happening to Him, and is well aware of the soldiers and the crowd that surrounds Him. He wasn't taken by surprise or feeling forsaken in the midst of it all. John reminds us: *"Jesus therefore, knowing all things that should come upon Him, went forth, and said unto them, Whom seek ye?"* (John 18:4).

He knew exactly what was happening to Him and knew all things that would happen to Him, including His impending death (see John 12:27). He knew all the things that would be done to Him and put into His hands by His Father: *"Jesus knowing that the Father had given all things into His hands, and that He was come from God…"* (John 13:3). This means He knew everything happening to Him and what would happen to Him soon, so there is no need to ask why. Again, just because the Scripture records Him saying a question doesn't mean He was asking one because He needed the answer. We will see that He was quoting a Scripture for the benefit of those that were there that day and future generations to follow.

We must remember that Jesus is naked, shamed before the people, He is numb with what feels like knives piercing through body and soul. Sure, He would feel forsaken and all alone. However, that doesn't mean He was questioning His Father about being forsaken. Isn't that how we feel when we are going through troubling times and painful trials? We tend to ask why and feel like God or no one cares or is even there for us? Yet Jesus is showing us that He is the answer, and also interceding for us and our questions of why.

In the midst of all this going on in His body and soul, Jesus would hold onto the promise of Abba never leaving His side. He wouldn't lose faith in His heavenly Daddy being there for Him and neither should we. So let's continue to see why Jesus made these remarks from the cross. Was Jesus telling the world that He was forsaken? Could He have been answering His critics, reminding them of a Messianic psalm written years before, foretelling of Him as the coming Messiah? Could He be telling them to rehearse Psalm 22 and reminding them that when He is lifted up, they will know who He is and that Abba is with Him (see John 8:28-32)! I believe this is exactly what He was doing. He was answering a question and giving hope to you, me, and all future generations.

Examining Psalm 22

In order to understand the answer to these questions and why Jesus was quoting from Psalm 22, we need to remember what was happening before He spoke this Scripture as if to ask a question. Of all the passages of Scripture, why would He say this one and why at this moment would He say it? In order to understand this, we then need to go back to some events prior to this statement He spoke from the cross.

As Jesus is suffering from the cross, many would shake their heads at Him, saying, "Jesus, You that said You would destroy the temple in three days; so save Yourself. If You are the Son of God, then come down from the cross and we will believe You. You saved others and You can't even save Yourself." Then they said, "He trusted in His Abba; let Him deliver Him now if He will have Him; for He said, 'I am the Son of God'" (see Ps. 22:8; Matt. 27:39-43).

The reason Jesus quotes Psalm 22, as if to ask a question of God or imply He was forsaken, was to answer those who were standing by the cross, mocking, laughing, and ridiculing Him while others were in deep sorrow.

Remember that He told them, "When you lift Me up to crucify Me, you will know who I am and that My Father is with Me." And this is exactly what He does. He gives them the answer to who He is by quoting a passage of Scripture: Psalm 22:1. He did this to reveal Abba and who He was to those that stood at the foot of the cross. Jesus was not asking God why or feeling forsaken, but He was quoting from the Psalms so these Jewish onlookers would know immediately what He was saying and would be reminded of what He told them. He was telling them that He was the One whom the psalmist David was writing about in Psalm 22.

In the Hebrew culture, when a person wanted his listeners to call to mind an entire psalm, it was the standard practice to merely quote the first few words of that psalm. It is a Jewish custom to know the psalm being quoted by the very first verses of it. For example, if you were to quote the first verse of Psalm 23, which is *"The Lord is my shepherd,"* then most would know immediately what specific psalm you were quoting and would even be able to tell you the contents and other verses in it.

We also can liken this same principle to simple songs today. If we sing a particular verse from a song, people know what song we are referring to. For example, "Twinkle, twinkle, little star," or "Mary had a little lamb," people know immediately the song being sung and can sing the rest of these songs with ease! Why is that? It is because we recognized the beginning verse. So just like Jesus quoting the first verse of Psalm 22, they would have known the entire psalm Jesus was referring to and what followed after!

So He quoted this to answer their questions of who He was and whether His Father would be with Him. This is why He immediately finds the energy to raise Himself up to quote it right after they question Him about who He is. For example, those doubting, by seeing Him on the cross, would also quote from the same psalm He would respond to them with:

> *All they that see Me laugh Me to scorn: they shoot out the lip, they shake the head, saying, He trusted on the Lord that He would deliver Him: let Him deliver Him, seeing He delighted in Him* (Psalm 22:7-8).

Then Jesus would follow up with their quote by identifying from the same psalm they referred to what was happening and what His heavenly Daddy would be doing. It would be to stay at His side! He doesn't argue with them, but rather reveals who He is and Abba's plan. They would further understand that that particular psalm teaches the suffering servant who wasn't forsaken on the cross, but God delivered him.

Psalm 22 reveals prophetically the real perspective of what was happening on the cross that day. These people would also remember the verses that mentioned they would pierce His hands and feet as they would look up at Jesus (see Ps. 22:16). They would be brought to remembrance of this same psalm as they saw the soldiers parting His garments (see Ps. 22:18). What better way for Jesus to identify who He was and what was happening by drawing attention to the same psalm by quoting the first verse in response to their disbelief and ridicule! We find this also in the same sequence of events recorded in Scripture. As they would question and mock Jesus, He would immediately answer with quoting Psalm 22 in response (see Matt. 27:39-46).

Defining Forsaken

We know He was crucified, but was He forsaken? When looking at the events of the cross that day, it helps to understand what the definition of *forsaken* means. With this in mind it takes on a whole new definition and understanding that He was not asking a question, but quoting Psalm 22 and making a statement that didn't have to do with being forsaken.

Let's consider the definition of *forsaken* since it is a word most never want to experience or think about. *Forsaken* in the Greek is *egkataleipó*, meaning "to separate connection with someone or something, forsake, abandon, or desert."[2] *Merriam-Webster's Dictionary* defines it as "to abandon (someone or something)," and "a tiny, forsaken island." It also goes on to define it as "to renounce or give up (something valued or pleasant)." The word *forsake* is an action word, meaning to renounce or turn away from entirely.

This is why Jesus told them beforehand, "My Father is with Me." Remember there was no relationship more intimate, personal, or important as the one with His heavenly Daddy. He would spend early mornings, all day, and even whole nights with His Abba in prayer. In public, He would mention His love and relationship with His Father, inviting others to know Him this way also. He would reveal that His Father was with Him at the tomb of His friend Lazarus, whom He would raise from the dead. He would show more intimacy and trust to His Abba than His friend Lazarus.

He would say that His Abba always hears Him (see John 11:42). If this is true, then His Father most certainly heard Him upon the cross. The basis of God forsaking somebody was usually if they would forsake Him then He would forsake them. This is why Second Chronicles 15:2 says, *"The Lord is with you, while ye be with Him; and if ye seek Him, He will be found of you; but if ye forsake Him, He will forsake you."*

So what does it matter if He was forsaken or not? After all, doesn't this give us hope if God forsook His Son, Jesus? Wouldn't this mean He would never forsake me because the Lord was forsaken in my place? Yes, Jesus, our Savior, died in our place and as the ultimate offering for sin. Yet it is not a requirement to have been forsaken by Abba or for Jesus to be forsaken in our place so we don't have to. Jesus was the offering for sin. He wasn't being offered so He would be forsaken so we wouldn't have to be. He was showing us that if God didn't forsake His Son, then He surely won't forsake us, no matter our pains, challenges, or sufferings in this life!

When we think of the Father forsaking Jesus, it can build a sense of fear and hopelessness within us. It doesn't add to the comfort of those who look to their heavenly Daddy for comfort, peace, and His faithfulness. This is because they think if He would forsake Jesus His Son, then maybe He will forsake them even though He said He wouldn't.

Isn't it more powerful, comforting, and loving for Abba not to forsake His Son and stay at His side then it is to forsake Him? What is the difference? If He would not forsake Jesus in all of the inhumane things He went through, then how much more comforting it is too know He won't forsake us! No matter what we are facing, suffering, hurting, or been through, if He was faithful to His Son, then we can take Him at His word that He won't forsake us either!

Here is our comfort as we see Abba remaining faithful to stay at Jesus's side. If God wouldn't forsake His Son, then how much more will He not forsake you and me! Through it all, Abba would be there for Jesus just like He was with Adam and Eve! He stood at His side and He will stand with you as well! He won't forsake you! His eye was on His Lamb and His eye is on you as we will see in the next chapter. This causes my heart to cry, "Abba!" How about you?

Notes

1. This definition is taken from *Strong's Concordance*, #912.
2. This definition is taken from *Strong's Concordance*, #1459.

Chapter Seven

Did Abba Turn Away?

For He hath not despised nor abhorred the affliction of the afflicted; neither hath He hid His face from him; but when he cried unto Him, He heard (Psalm 22:24).

Abba is watching intensely as His eye is upon His only begotten Son, Jesus. The heavenly Father has remained faithful to be at His side. His Father's heart is feeling the pain, the sorrow, and the love for His Son who has become the offering of all sin. Abba is aware of His suffering and listening to the words of Jesus from the cross. He hears His words of forgiveness directed toward others. He listens as His Son thirsts, and smiles with approval as He watches Jesus reach out to the two thieves at His side.

Abba's heart has been engaged in the events that are transpiring. He is feeling every bit of pain, hurt, and suffering that His Son is experiencing. He has to look past His own feelings and allow His plan to be carried out exactly as He determined. He knows this is what He and His Son had agreed upon before the foundations of the earth were made. It was to create a family in Their image, and the fulfillment of this plan was happening at this very moment. They were united and committed to see it fulfilled, especially after Adam and Eve had sinned and needed a Savior to redeem them and all mankind. Abba's faith has not been shaken and He is delighted in His Son's obedience. He knows the outcome of this unfair, unjust treatment of His Son. Yet there is no choice for this to cease; it has to be, there is no one else but His beloved Son who can pay this price and fulfill the ultimate plan to save the human race.

He is grieved in His heart as onlookers stand at the foot of the cross, not understanding that there is no greater love than what they are witnessing. It is for His Son to lay down His life willingly as He is now. Abba listens to their words that are rejecting this sinless offering that would save them. Jesus is giving His very life, taking their sins, sickness, diseases, pains, and suffering upon Himself so they could be forgiven, saved, and healed. Yet, rather than call upon His Son or believe Him, they ridicule Him, doubt Him, and even think that Abba has left His Son. Don't they understand this agreement between Father and Son, and the words that His Son revealed that He wouldn't be alone? Those comforting words He spoke ahead of His crucifixion that His heavenly Daddy would be with Him, even though it would appear He is alone, are truly powerful.

Abba knows that Jesus is strong in His heart even though His muscles are contracting, cramping, and there is nonstop, relentless throbbing pain throughout His whole body. His chest muscles are burning and paralyzed as He tries to draw air into His lungs, but can't exhale. The Father would do anything to put His hands under His Son's shoulders to hold Him and support Him, especially as Jesus has to use every ounce of energy just to push Himself up so He can breathe, let alone speak. This is the result of hours of suffering that have now set in. It is now the "ninth hour" of the day, which would be three o'clock in the afternoon. By this time, Jesus had been on the cross for six excruciating hours. Yet the Son of God finds the energy to shout something loudly—but why loudly? Why shout it? Can't His Father hear Him?

With a Loud Voice

At the ninth hour Jesus shouts with a loud voice, saying, "Eloi, Eloi, lama sabachthani? which is, being interpreted, My God, my God, why hast Thou forsaken Me?" (Mark 15:34; see Ps. 22:1).

Abba is with Him, and He hears His Son, so there is no need to shout. Why not whisper it between Father and Son? After all, by shouting aren't you adding fuel to their accusations that You are alone, Jesus, and that Your Father is not there to help You? Isn't this furthering their claims accusing You of not being the Son of God? This is why this loud cry was not a question, but a statement Jesus was making. He doesn't have to shout it, but He does so in order to make sure those watching Him suffer hear Him.

His heavenly Daddy can hear a whisper from His mouth. He can hear the cry of His heart and our heart without the opening our mouths. He surely knows God heard the prayer of Hannah in the Bible who only whispered her prayer and He answered by giving her a son, Samuel the prophet. So there is no need to shout; but Jesus does! This is not a cry for God to hear, but a loud cry because men needed to hear Him.

It is to remind the people who He is, and for all hell to tremble as their celebration of Jesus being crucified is interrupted. Jesus purposely made sure that those standing by would hear Him, thus the reason for Him to let His onlookers hear exactly what He was saying with every ounce of energy He had, crying out with a loud voice.

It was to build faith in those who loved and believed Him and in those who didn't so they would know who He truly was. Jesus wanted them to realize that He was in fact the Messiah who offered Himself willingly as sin's sacrifice. They had done all they could to His body that He gave and they had done all they could to attack His soul. However, what they couldn't do was break His spirit. His spirit was strong as we see by Him crying out with a loud voice. He shouted it so they could hear it. It was by Jesus's loud cry that He was showing them that His spirit was strong even though they had done all they could to Him. They couldn't touch His spirit, for His heart belonged to His heavenly Daddy, and He trusted Him. He was committed to Abba and Abba was committed to Him. He wasn't saying it for His benefit but for the people to know that God was with Him. He was declaring that His spirit remained strong and not one of feeling forsaken. He was dedicated to His Father's plan to restore mankind to Abba through His death. It was in the natural, visible world that Jesus was being tortured and at the same time in the spiritual, invisible Kingdom He was in Abba's care.

This cry Jesus was making from the cross is not one of being forsaken as we discussed earlier; it is a message to let them know that His heavenly Daddy has heard Him. This shout is not for Jesus's or Abba's benefit, but for ours. It is to encourage us that we don't have to ever feel or think we are forsaken when we have Abba as our Father and Jesus as our Lord. He was giving an answer of hope and comfort to all mankind. He shouted it so that everyone would know precisely what was transpiring. That powerful shout shattered the teeth of the wicked and loosened mankind from the clutches of the devil who wants men to feel lost and forsaken without God. What better way than to answer the skeptics and give hope to others by drawing their attention to the verse He was quoting from Psalm 22. It would be in that psalm that we would get a glimpse of what was prophetically taking place from Jesus's perspective and where His Abba was.

In Psalm 22 we see what was taking place as David prophetically wrote this psalm. It shows what is happening not only in King David's life but what would also reveal Abba and Jesus together in the events of the crucifixion for our benefit! It is a mixture of David's struggle and is prophetic for the crucifixion. It was to not only show what was happening in his life, but to foretell the Messiah's suffering on the cross. David's identification with this psalm and Jesus referring to it doesn't make the words of this psalm any less true.

Even though it is a Messianic psalm, these words spoken by the Lord at the time of His crucifixion were penned by David many years before. Crying with a loud voice, saying, *"My God, My God, why hast Thou forsaken Me?"* (Ps. 22:1), Jesus is actually quoting the first verse of this psalm, which identifies one who is asking why he is being forsaken. This is not to be confused with David's own feeling of being forsaken in this same psalm, who in the remaining passages finds help from his God after all. We must not forget in this psalm, whether it is in David's life or Jesus's on the cross, that they both do in fact receive help from God in the time of their affliction.

Let's look at Psalm 22 more closely. It will help us better understand why Jesus quoted loudly the first verse of this psalm from the cross. In this psalm, we find many prophetic parallels to what Jesus was experiencing on the cross.

"My God, My God, Why have You forsaken Me?" (Ps. 22:1 NIV): There are some important things to observe about this verse. Jesus's utterance of this statement is only mentioned in Matthew and Mark's Gospels, but is not included in Luke's or John's. Perhaps this is because the emphasis was not on Jesus being forsaken, but instead referencing this psalm for His hearers so they would understand the significance of the event.

As we have mentioned, it doesn't necessarily mean that Jesus was calling unto His Father, saying, "My God, My God…" because He was asking a question, but He was rather quoting this psalm to let those who were mocking and doubting know who He truly was!

Did you ever notice that Jesus's quote and statement of this verse is not "My Abba," or "My Father, why have You forsaken Me?" This is important to see because whenever Jesus addressed God from the cross, it was always in reference to Him being Jesus's Father or God.

> *Then said Jesus, Father, forgive them; for they know not what they do* (Luke 23:34).

> *And when Jesus had cried with a loud voice, He said, Father, into Thy hands I commend My spirit: and having said thus, He gave up the ghost* (Luke 23:46).

This is why these words from Jesus on the cross were not addressing His Abba with a question, but simply making a statement. It is further why *God* is used instead of *Father* because it was not addressed to Him per se, but for the people to understand. Notice the other parallels to what Jesus was experiencing from this psalm that point to the event of the cross.

- *"But I am a worm and not a man, scorned by men and despised by the people"* (Ps. 22:6 NIV): The word *worm* is the Hebrew word *tola*, which is not the ordinary word for worm. Rather, this was a worm from which crimson or scarlet dye was obtained. This particular use of worm was used because Jesus was covered with blood, and that was the color of scarlet dye.

- *"Many bulls surrounded me; strong bulls of Bashan encircle me"* (Ps. 22:12 NIV): What does Bashan have to do with anything? It was the chief cattle-raising area of Israel where the biggest, best, and strongest bulls came from. The bulls represent the religious leaders fierce rejection of Jesus as Messiah and the Roman guards who crucified him.

- *"I am poured out like water, and all my bones are out of joint: my heart is like wax; it is melted in the midst of my bowels"* (Ps. 22:14): This is describing Jesus's heart and what He was feeling in His body from the things He was suffering while upon the cross.

- *"Dogs have surrounded me; a band of evil men has encircled me, they have pierced my hands and my feet"* (Ps. 22:16 NIV): The *dogs* spoken of here are the Gentile Roman guards.

- *"They part my garments among them, and cast lots upon my vesture"* (Ps. 22:18): This is evident from the fact that the soldiers did cast lots for Jesus's clothing.

- *"Deliver my life from the sword, my precious life from the power of the dogs. Rescue me from the mouth of the lions; save me from the horns of the wild oxen* (Ps. 22:20-21 NIV): The *dogs* are again referring to Romans, the mouth of the lions speaks of the Pharisees, the religious leaders of that time, while the horns of wild oxen would be Gentile enemies of the Messiah. The masses of Jewish people followed Jesus, it was the Jewish leaders whose kingdom was threatened that rejected Him.

These verses describe what Jesus was going through and prophesying of what is happening as He is hanging on the cross. Men scorn Him as He hangs in shame. His heart melts like wax from the things He is suffering. His hands and feet are pierced and nailed to the cross. The soldiers are gambling for His clothes. But in all of this, we find that Abba is still with Him.

This psalm is often quoted from the first verse alone or with a few verses that we referenced. However, there is a vital verse that is often not mentioned when the first verse is so often quoted. It, too, reveals that God didn't abandon His Son or turn His face from Him.

If we are going to refer to this psalm as a Messianic psalm depicting the events of the crucifixion, then we can't only mention the first verse Jesus quoted from the cross, excluding this important verse. It says Abba will *not* hide His face from Jesus's cry for help or, for that matter, from the sinner's cry for help! As we mentioned in this same psalm, what seemed like being forsaken turns out to be that God was in fact present with Him.

> *For He hath not despised nor abhorred the affliction of the afflicted; neither hath He hid His face from Him; but when He cried unto Him, He heard* (Psalm 22:24).

As we see from this verse, Jesus wasn't despised, abhorred, and God didn't hide His face from Him. His heavenly Father heard Him! He didn't turn His face away, but He heard Him from the cross of suffering and shame. This is why Jesus quoted the first verse of this psalm in a loud voice, as we have mentioned previously. He wanted His hearers to know what His mission was and that His Abba was with Him. They would recognize this psalm and further remember the rest of the verses that go along with it, especially verse 24, which said God didn't hide His face from Him, but heard Him!

With a loud voice from the cross, Jesus was saying, "Let the whole world know I am not forsaken! My Abba has not despised or turned away from My suffering, pain, or trouble. He has not hidden His face from Me but has heard My words from the cross! I am not alone and neither will be mankind."

This meant there would now be mercy given, peace on earth, and goodwill toward all men. It was to cause Satan to tremble and the earth to shake! This is because something is happening that is restoring hope to the hopeless, peace to the broken, healing to the afflicted, and forgiveness to the sinner. Abba and His Son are fulfilling the plan given to man for our benefit! The family of God is being restored and the lost created children of Abba can come home. This is why the union between Abba and Jesus is not being broken.

God Looked Upon Christ

It is important to know this union between them. They would not be separated. When Jesus was dying on the cross, the Scriptures say that God was in Christ, reconciling the world to Himself, no longer counting people's sin against them (see 2 Cor. 5:19). If God was in Christ reconciling the world unto Himself as Jesus was being crucified, then how could He have left Him while He was on the cross?

The message given from the cross is not one of turning away, but rather of looking upon His Son to satisfy Abba's righteous and justified anger that was intended for man. This is because we were guilty of sin and had disobeyed. Yet, mercy has triumphed over judgment; love has prevailed over sin as the Son of God has given Himself in our place. This is also why it has pleased His Father to allow Him to be afflicted, to be wounded for our transgressions, and bruised for our iniquities. He took for us the chastisement and the punishment of our sins upon Him so we could be healed and forgiven (see Isa. 53). Abba's eyes were upon His Lamb and would not turn away from Him, now being focused upon us and all who will come unto Him.

How comforting and reassuring it is to know from this psalm, that in the midst of the Messiah's suffering, He was not turned away from by His heavenly Daddy. This is important for us to know because it reaffirms that we are loved and accepted by God also. It is why there is comfort in knowing the meaning behind what Jesus meant when He shouted this statement loudly from the cross. It also helps to let us know our heavenly Daddy is committed to us. He was committed to His Son, which gave Abba access back to mankind so He could be our heavenly Daddy also. We are not alone because God wants to be with us in the same way He was with His Son. He is Emmanuel, God with us. Isn't that what was said regarding our precious Savior's birth?

How comforting and reassuring it is to know we are loved and not condemned by God. People need to know this because it helps them understand how He feels about them and that they are accepted and not forsaken by Him. When people feel lonely or abandoned, they often think God has left them as well. This is why it is often hard for people to relate to God as a heavenly Daddy, let alone call Him Abba. It is because they question whether anyone cares, let alone God. Yet He does care more than we'll ever imagine! He showed it in His actions toward His Son for our benefit!

We must not let our trials and tribulations keep us from Abba's love. There is no greater love than what Abba and Jesus displayed on our behalf! Our lack of understanding concerning this may keep us from receiving our heavenly Daddy's many benefits! It can keep us from being blessed by God, healed, delivered, or even touched by Him. This is not because these things are not available for us. We know Jesus paid the price so they are freely given and available. We can hinder these blessings, however, because of our own feelings of doubt, failure, or unworthiness.

Never forget that Abba has His eyes upon us and is concerned for our every need.

Calling for Elijah?

Shaking their fists in the air and hurling insults toward Jesus, some of the crowd would continue their constant berating of Him at the foot of the cross and as they would walk by. "You saved others; now save Yourself," they would say. In the same way, the scribes and chief priests would further mock Him, saying, "If You truly are the Son of God, let Him save You. Come down from the cross so we will believe." If that wasn't bad enough, Jesus was getting literally accused on every side! He had those at His feet and one of the thieves at His side continuing to speak great words of hate, mocking and ridiculing Him.

Jesus was the Suffering Servant who would not argue with them but rather, as we have said, lift His voice for all to hear. His words of *"Eloi, Eloi, lama sabathani,"* would cause some of them to pause and listen to what He was saying. Mark says, *"When some of those standing near heard this, they said, 'Listen, He's calling Elijah'"* (Mark 15:35 NIV). Their hearts were so hard and darkened that some actually thought Jesus was calling on the prophet Elijah to help Him. This shouldn't be surprising, especially when they denied that He was the Son of God and that He came from His Father. However, something powerful and prophetic was also taking place!

The curse of sin was being broken through Jesus Christ. It was a known fact that those being crucified were considered cursed. It is, as the Scripture says of Jesus being crucified, that He was made a curse for us because cursed is every man that hangs on a tree (see Gal. 3:13-14). Yet, Jesus became this curse by willingly offering Himself to die so that God's plan spoken to Adam and Eve and promised to Abraham and his children would be fulfilled. This is why the prophetic significance of them thinking that Jesus was calling out for Elijah it not a coincidence. They didn't understand what was happening from their statement and needed prophetic ears to hear and hearts to understand. They didn't realize their associating of Jesus on the cross and thinking He was calling for Elijah were prophetically connected—and that it affects us today. Why is this?

It is because it further reveals Abba's plan fulfilled and His heart to restore His family back to Him. It was breaking a curse that had been on the earth that Jesus was paying the price for—the curse of separation between God and man, and the resulting separation of families. This is what the prophet Malachi spoke about, a future restoration that would come from the spirit of Elijah that would restore the hearts of the fathers to their children and the children to their fathers (see Mal. 4:6). God and His children being reconciled through Jesus's death fulfilled this prophecy! Not only that, but the curse that is upon the earth that is breaking up families and dividing fathers from their children will be broken through Jesus Christ and all those who call upon Him.

This is why the statement Jesus made on the cross, quoting the first verse of Psalm 22, is for those who have prophetic ears to hear and a heart to understand. It would reveal that there would no longer be separation between God and man. The heart of Abba is restored to His children because of Jesus's purposeful, righteous actions to bear sin's burden for us. This curse is broken; there is no more need to be separated from Abba or to be separated in our homes or families any longer. We don't have to be separated from God's great love! We don't have to allow the devil to break up our families or live with the feelings of being alienated from God any longer. We can experience the blessings over our lives and families through a life committed to Jesus Christ and our heavenly Daddy.

It is through Christ that the curse upon families has been broken. The bond that wasn't broken between Abba and His

Son is evidence it doesn't have to be broken between fathers and sons or parents and children today. We don't have to become hopeless victims of broken homes or relationships. If this has happened in our lives, we now have hope because that curse is broken through the sacrifice of Jesus. It doesn't have to be a part of our lives if we believe and receive the benefits of reconciliation and restoration that come through Jesus and our heavenly Daddy. This means that if these things have happened in our lives, Abba is there for us to give us a hope, a future, and an expected end.

This horrible separation from God, our Abba, doesn't have to be for anyone born into the earth. It is through our acceptance of His Son, Jesus, that we are reborn and adopted as His dear children! This means that what Jesus did for us on the cross is complete; it is finished! It's over and is paid for in full! We don't have to live a life full of sickness, disease, poverty, bondage, brokenness, and despair, to name but a few.

Do you know why? It's because Jesus paid for them all and even declared that His actions of dying on the cross made it complete. We don't have to live a life without God and without hope in this sinful world. We don't have to live under the curse of sin but rather in the blessings of Abba! Why? Because as Jesus said, "It is finished!" The victory belongs to the Lord and has now become ours today through Him and a life committed to His Kingdom.

It Is Finished

Once again, this cry of "My God, My God, why have You forsaken Me?" would prove to those that were present at Jesus's last moments upon this earth that He is the true Lamb of God, the promised Messiah. As we referenced before, Jesus was quoting the first verse of this psalm to preach a sermon to His listeners. But at the end of Psalm 22 is a verse that announces it is complete and finished.

Jesus would thirst from the cross, but then speak His final words addressing His Abba. He would shout with a loud voice, saying, "Abba, Father, it is finished; into Your hands I give My spirit." Jesus was again drawing attention to Psalm 22, quoting the fulfillment of this prophecy right before their very eyes. Notice that His statement was the last words of this same psalm we have been discussing: *"They shall come and shall declare His righteousness to a people yet to be born—that He has done it [that it is finished]!"* (Ps. 22:31 AMP).

Jesus was saying with this announcement that it was complete: "You didn't do this because you can't save yourself! I, as the Son of Man and the Son of God, did this for you: it is now finished!" This is a further indication of what Jesus was trying to communicate by quoting this verse loudly and being mistaken by others as Him calling out for Elijah.

Jesus had completed the plan of God and gave the opportunity for mankind to be restored back into His family. This was shown by the two thieves on the cross and that reconciliation with Abba was available to whomever would call upon God to receive it. There were two thieves that were also crucified with the Lord. Yet, one cursed Jesus, refusing to believe in Him! Therefore, he was never reconciled to Abba through Jesus in his last living moments. However, the other thief told him to quit railing on Jesus and even called upon the Lord, asking Him to remember him when He enters into paradise. We know that this thief actually did receive eternal life and to this day is with Jesus, reconciled to His heavenly Daddy. This example of the two thieves prophetically shows the restoration of Abba with His children.

It is exactly what takes place today among those who call upon His name. There are those who reject God and those who will call upon Him to be saved! You see, the thief that rejected the Lord, sadly represents those who refuse to believe or call out to the Lord in order to be saved from their sins. They will never reconcile with their Creator or ever come to know Abba through Jesus. The other thief speaks of those who turn their life over to Jesus and call upon Him to be saved. They give their life and eternal state to Him. Once they do this, they are reconciled back to Abba forever.

Abba didn't forsake Jesus on the cross and neither would Jesus forsake the thief who called upon Him to be saved from his sins! This shows us that Jesus is the answer for every one and every family! We must call upon Him to be saved and have access to Abba!

God Dwells in Darkness

Thank God it is finished and will forever remain completed by what Jesus did through His death and resurrection. He suffered on the cross, was buried, then raised on the third day. Jesus won the victory over sin and death for us! We can now live in the blessings of God and not under the curse of sin. We can call upon Abba at any time, even in our last moments on earth, much like the thief on the cross. However, some today sadly refuse to include Abba in their lives and won't call upon Him no matter what situation they are in. Instead, they decide to live under the darkness of sin and its consequences. This is the reason that some feel alienated or forsaken of God because of the darkness and lifestyle they choose. Since Jesus died on the cross, we don't have to live in darkness any longer. He made it possible so we can live in the victory of righteousness!

When people choose darkness, life becomes confusing, frightening, and can even cause us not to discern God correctly. We see this same effect darkness has upon people by looking at the last few hours on the cross as Jesus announced that it was finished. It will help us to see that just because it seems dark in our lives, or maybe we are facing attacks from the enemy and feel as though we have blown it, the Lord has not turned away, forsaking us, but wants us to include Him in our lives!

The Bible says that darkness covered the earth as Jesus hung there in the final hours of His life. This darkness is so thick that it can be literally felt by those that look on the events of the crucifixion. It is so dark that it penetrates the very atmosphere for three hours. This is unusual seeing it is only the afternoon, but great darkness hovers over the earth and this divine light of the world, Jesus. Yet, in the midst of darkness Abba has His eye on His Lamb, His very own Son. In the same way in our times of struggles, He will keep a watchful eye upon us because He cares for us and knows when we are suffering, in pain, and facing challenges. This is why it is vital to understand that He kept His eye on His Son. We can now rest in that same assurance that He will be committed to us in the same way He was committed to His Son.

The darkness that was upon the earth at that time, what does it mean? That He was forsaken? Abandoned? That God is now turning His face away from Jesus? This darkness was not only all of hell partaking of the events of the crucifixion, but it was also the gross, heavy darkness of all men's sins that Jesus was suffering for as sin's sacrifice.

The Bible doesn't give any natural reason for why there was darkness upon the whole earth. One such reason for it was to remind the people of God's deliverance and His commitment of sending the promised Messiah. This is why Jesus died during the Feast of Passover, which was a very important holy holiday for the Jews. When the darkness came during this religious holiday, no doubt they would associate it to the time when God rescued their ancestors from Egypt during the first Passover.

It was to remind the people that it was in darkness that God would deal with Pharaoh, Israel's enemy. It was also to remind them that God delivered them and gave them victory after years of cruel and hard bondage.

This is exactly what was happening with Jesus hanging on the cross in utter darkness. God was dealing with the sin of the people and with their enemy, the devil. He was delivering them from sin and the hand of the enemy into a life of blessing and victory. This darkness was a sign of God's punishment against the enemy and His displeasure with sin. It was also to be a reminder that He shows up and intervenes in the midst of darkness.

Does this darkness reveal that God turns away and removes His presence from Jesus's suffering? After all, this is how people often feel when facing life's challenges. It is also how people perceive Jesus's loud cry from the cross, "My God, My God, why have You forsaken Me?" We have to understand that just because it is dark doesn't mean it is void of God's presence. How do we know this? Because God can be found in darkness and often shows up when it is the darkest in our lives. Consider how God came to speak with Moses and meet with the children of Israel before they were about to enter the Promised Land: *"And you came near and stood at the foot of the mountain, and the mountain burned with fire to the heart of heaven, with darkness, cloud, and thick gloom"* (Deut. 4:11 AMP).

Notice how God appeared to Moses in a dark and thick cloud. Moses would spend time with God in His presence that came as thick darkness (see Exod. 20:21). That's how the Lord showed up to meet with Moses. So just because it was dark during this time on the cross doesn't mean God's presence wasn't there with Jesus.

Another example of God showing up in darkness is the pillar of cloud by day and the fire by night. This cloud of darkness and fire was a light and protection to Israel but became darkness to Pharaoh and his pursuing army (see Exod. 14). The people experiencing the effects of darkness can see an important truth. It depended on Israel's perspective and what side of the cloud they were on. It was the same dark cloud that punished Pharaoh and his armies; yet, at the same time, this dark cloud contained God's presence and blessed and protected Israel, showing them He didn't forsake them.

It is in much the same way that darkness came at the time of Jesus's suffering on the cross and as He spoke His final words. It was darkness against the enemy and all his hordes of hell. It was darkness to those in sin and to those caught in spiritual darkness. Yet, it was a dark cloud of His presence that hovered over the precious Lamb of God that would take away the sins of the world!

God does and can manifest Himself in darkness. He did it in the temple with Solomon and the priests. Solomon immediately explains His glory cloud as being dark:

> So that the priests could not stand to minister by reason of the cloud: for the glory of the Lord had filled the house of God. Then said Solomon, The Lord hath said that He would dwell in the thick darkness (2 Chronicles 5:14–6:1).

The darkness that appeared for those few hours during the crucifixion doesn't indicate abandonment by Abba! It doesn't mean He turned His face as to not look at His suffering Son either. He was just as much involved in Jesus's sufferings and the state of mankind in the midst of the thick darkness as He was in the days when He blessed the people of Israel and defeated the enemy during the first Passover. So we need to be encouraged that just because it was dark, or just because it may seem difficult and dark in our own lives, doesn't mean God is not there to help us or hear us when we cry unto Him.

I am not implying that God never turned His face from people in Scripture, as we know in certain times He did. Yet, on the cross, we can conclude that Abba did in fact hear His Son when He called out and didn't abandon Him! Just because it was dark didn't mean that God was unable to look at Jesus because of the horrible sins of all mankind that were upon Him. This is vital for us to know because sometimes when we blow it, the devil is always there to tell us that somehow God has left us and He now can't look at us. The result is that it leaves us with a sense of shame and feelings of unworthiness. Abba kept His eyes on Jesus through His suffering to show you that He will keep His eye on you if you allow Him and live a life committed to Him.

It is often suggested that God can't look at sin, so this was the reason that it was dark while Jesus was being crucified. Again, does this mean that Abba turned His face from Jesus and He couldn't look upon sin? To answer these questions further, we first need to remember that God gave Jesus over to allow men to crucify Him. This didn't mean that God turned away, but rather allowed Him to be punished for our sakes. This punishment wasn't an unkind or unjust action from Abba. No man would take Jesus's life because He would offer it willingly as part of what He agreed to do concerning His Father's plan. Abba didn't give Jesus any special favor or advantage by avoiding suffering. Jesus couldn't take a shortcut by bypassing any trial in the work of redemption. This was so no one could imply that He had some unfair advantage by His Father.

Can God Look at Sin?

So, can God look at sin? We know He did look at sin when He stared at Jesus hanging on the cross. He stared straight at it while Jesus was paying for all sin. We know this from the 24th verse of Psalm 22 as we mentioned before: *"For He has not turned away from the suffering of the one in pain or trouble. He has not hidden His face from him. But He has heard his cry for help"* (Ps. 22:24 NLV).

The reason people often believe that God can't look at sin is because He is so holy and therefore can't look upon it. Yes, He is holy—we know that without question. But, yes, He can look at sin. Let's think for a moment if God could not look at sin and if He turned away from Jesus when it was dark. The questions we need to ask are at what point did He stop looking at Jesus on the cross? At what point, during that horrific crucifixion, did Abba then find it now acceptable and possible to resume looking at His Son again? Was it because at a certain moment the sin disappeared from His swollen, bruised, and bloodied body, making it now pleasing to look upon His Son again?

This kind of interpretation is often based on a passage in the Bible that says that the people's iniquities have caused a separation between them and God, and their sins have hid His face from them (see Isa. 59:2). This verse is often used to suggest that it means that He could not look upon Jesus on the cross because of the iniquity laid upon Him. What this verse is saying is that God doesn't endorse, tolerate, or look upon their sin favorably. It is not saying that He can't or doesn't look at iniquity, but rather He has chosen not to look at it. Therefore, it should not be used to compare the events on the cross and whether or not Abba can look at sin.

It is again implied that God can't look at sin from some verses in the writings of Habakkuk. They are often related to the events on the cross that support the idea of Abba turning away from Jesus because He can't look at sin. Habakkuk writes, *"Your eyes are too pure to look at sin. You cannot look on wrong. Why then do You look with favor on those who do wrong?"* (Hab. 1:13 NLV). We can understand from this verse that Habakkuk is making a statement as to why God is in fact looking at sin.

He was saying, "God, Your eyes are too pure to look upon evil and You don't tolerate wrong, so then why are You looking at it?" It made no sense to Habakkuk as to why God was looking on sin when he believed that it wasn't possible.

But this is exactly what people do when they interpret the events of the cross and how God deals with people today. They jump to rash judgments when something goes wrong that it is God turning away or judging that person because of their sin. They treat people as though their sin is so deplorable that not even God is looking upon them. Maybe this is why evangelism in the church is often not made a priority? However, God does look upon sin and does love the sinner. This is not to give people a freedom or endorsement for a life of sin, but rather if one is struggling with sin and wants to change, then they need to know God doesn't approve of their sin but is still there for them. And this is also why it is important not to treat this verse in Habakkuk as a question, but rather as a statement he was making. He is not stating that God cannot look at sin. He is asking God for clarification.

Now please don't misunderstand me: sin can bring a barrier between God's presence and our lives if we allow it to. It can then cause Him to turn His face in the sense of allowing us to continue in our sin, with His desire for us to change (see Rom. 1). Remember that the turning of His face doesn't necessarily mean being forsaken or abandoned, just like with Jesus on the cross. What sin does is interferes with His presence and the dynamics of God in our lives. This is because we sense the Lord's heart is not pleased concerning our sin, knowing He doesn't approve of it. So, as a result, it interferes with our fellowship with Him.

For some it causes them to avoid time with Him because of the guilt of their sins, so they avoid the deeper life with Abba. Others try to ignore dealing with the sin in their lives, hoping it will go away or God will approve of it in time; but the fact is that when this happens people start adjusting more to the pleasures of their flesh then pleasing God in righteousness. This is what happened when Adam and Eve hid from God's presence because of sin, thus forever changing the dynamics of their relationship with Him. They didn't consider God's heart in the matter and took things into their own hands by establishing in their minds their own standard of righteousness by making fig leaves to cover their nakedness.

Sadly, some think today you shouldn't talk about living a life of righteousness because we are all under grace. Yes, we are under grace! But it is suggested that a change of lifestyle is putting them under the law of sin consciousness. We need to understand that just because we are under grace doesn't mean we have a license to sin or to get loose with sin. It is not simply ignoring a standard of righteousness or exempting us of all talk of righteous living. We are told to live holy as He is holy (see 1 Pet. 1:16).

It is not cheap grace when we have accountability to God for our actions in life, or self-examination. The Scripture tells us many times throughout the New Testament to examine ourselves (see 1 Cor. 11:28-30; Gal. 6:3-4). This isn't self-condemnation or being so afraid to sin or make a mistake because Abba will punish us, but rather being aware of how we are living in God's sight. Is it pleasing to God and a testimony before men? Is it a pure life that seeks God and does what is right? This isn't sin consciousness, but being conscious of not grieving the Holy Spirit with our actions. It is being conscious that we must let our light shine before men that they may see our good works and glorify God. It is being conscious that we are to live as Christ did in righteousness and not in unrighteousness, cheapening the work of grace. The Bible tells us that we can fail the grace of God through our sinful, hardened hearts and unrepentant life (see Heb. 12:15)! We shouldn't continue to live a life of sin and think that grace will abound, for even the Scripture says, "God forbid!" (see Rom. 6:1-2).

Let's consider further what sin consciousness or lack of grace is by looking at Jesus's address to the seven churches in the Book of Revelation. He pointed out their sins, bringing attention to their lifestyles. He made them conscious of their sin and wrong-doings by telling them they needed to examine themselves. He even demanded and expected that they repent (see Rev. 2–3). This wasn't putting them under the law, but giving them the opportunity to adjust the way they were living so they could enjoy the benefits of His grace. The same is true for us today. Yes, we are under grace, and yes, Abba's eyes are on us and we are accepted by Him. He is with us as He was with His Son. But we need to live a life that exemplifies that truth.

Abba can look at sin and He did as Jesus hung from the cross. He does this so He can reach out to us in His mercy and grace, giving us the opportunity to change. He doesn't want us to live in the darkness of sin but in the light of His truth and blessings.

There are many times throughout Scripture where God looked at sin. He saw the sin of Adam and Eve, who covered themselves with fig leaves, but it was God who reached out to them. He cut covenant with a pagan man named Abraham. He used Moses, who murdered a man, to deliver His people from Egypt. He restored King David after committing adultery with Bathsheba and having her husband murdered. He had a conversation with the most deplorable, wicked entity in existence, Lucifer, who came to His throne to discuss a righteous man named Job. God also looked at sin when He looked at the thief on the cross.

The fact is that God can look upon sin and it doesn't affect Him. He doesn't look at it as a mean, heavenly Daddy, but rather as a loving forgiving, merciful, and righteous Father who longs to help us. He knows the terrible effects of sin and how it can cause the devil to have access to His children as a result. It opens us up to dangerous consequences. It can hurt our bodies and our minds. It can destroy marriages, families, children, and society. This is why Abba must look at sin, so as to intervene as the answer of light to a dark world.

In the days of the prophet Jeremiah, God didn't turn His face away, but stared right at the sin of the people, ready to judge it after seeing how detestable it was. God said, *"For Mine eyes are upon all their ways: they are not hid from My face, neither is their iniquity hid from Mine eyes"* (Jer. 16:17).

We don't have to be enslaved to sin or live a shameful life of secret sin. We have victory over sin and the works of darkness through Jesus Christ! We need to be encouraged that through the finished work of the cross, sin has been defeated! Living a life that is pure is one of the great honors that we give to the Lord. Sin disappoints Him and can anger Him as well. It hurts Him and grieves Him. When we desire to do what is right in His eyes, it pleases Him. We do this because we love Him and honor Him. God hates sin because of what it does to us, not because it is so bad that He can't look at it.

God looks at sin more so today because of the sinful world we live in. Thank God through Jesus we have the answer to true peace on earth. Through Jesus goodwill is available toward all men if they will receive it. God's grace abounds! This is because love, peace, and forgiveness were injected in the earth through Jesus. God the Father, even though He can and does look at sin, sees it through a different element—the blood of Jesus!

God now sees us through the blood of His Son that was shed for a ransom for many. This means we have immediate access to Him when we sin. We can come to Abba and ask Him to forgive us and help us live a life that is pleasing to Him. It is because of the grace of God made available through Jesus's shed blood that we aren't turned away from His mercy or forgiveness.

Think for a moment if God couldn't look at sin? There would be no hope for mankind to be saved or mercy and forgiveness. It is often said that God doesn't hear you after you've sinned. This again is often compared to the darkness that came at the time Jesus was crying out from the cross. They say it was to reveal that God didn't hear Jesus at that moment because of the sin that He was bearing. However, as we saw, God heard His Son in the midst of paying the price for the sin of all mankind. God heard Jesus then and He hears us now.

We need to ask ourselves a question: If God can't hear us if we sin, then how is He going to hear if someone calls upon Him to be saved? Wasn't it God who heard the cries of repentance from those in Nineveh, just as much as He heard the thief's cry for help next to Him on the cross? The reason God often doesn't hear our prayers when we are living in sin isn't because sin has some great power over Him; it is because of what sin does to *us*—it hardens our hearts by the sinful paths we choose and makes His voice harder to hear. Abba is speaking to us, reaching out to us, but we often listen with our fingers in our ears. Sin hardens our hearts, developing selective hearing, and as a result we do our own will and not His.

So God will sometimes allow us to walk down a certain path as He did with the prodigal son who foolishly lived it up with a rebellious life of sin (see Luke 15). But in the end, the loving father waited for the son to come to a place where he was dissatisfied with the way he was living, finally realizing there was a better life available than sin, and so returning to his loving father. This is exactly what Abba has to do because of the choices of some. It is not that He has turned away, but He lets us choose what manner of person we want to be. Do we, like the prodigal son, want to live a life of compromise, carnality, worldliness, or a life under the pleasing hand and care of our Abba in righteousness? This usually happens after many attempts from His compassionate care as our heavenly Daddy. He tries to get our attention, intervening in our lives, and calling us to a way of honor before Him.

I want us to understand that by saying God can look at sin isn't to diminish the awfulness of sin or lessen the extreme ugliness of the sins that Jesus was bearing on the cross. Neither am I implying that Abba is some harsh dictatorial judge that is ready to react at every wrong move we make. What I'm saying is that God is holy and righteous and does *not* look at sin with favor. He sees our sins, yet He still loves us and reaches out to us in the midst of our sin. This is why there is comfort in that Abba didn't turn away from His Son as sin's sacrifice.

We certainly know that God is holy, but if sin is what made Him turn away from Jesus, then what hope is there for us? When it came to the payment of sin from His Son concerning our sins, what difference would there be between one sin and all sin that Jesus was paying for? The amount of sin or sin itself doesn't give Abba a reason to forsake His Son or look away.

We often think that sin is somehow a threat to His holiness. But this would mean He would have to turn away to preserve His own holiness or goodness. Abba is both truth and light. And in His presence darkness must flee, not the other way around.

God can look upon sin and would look upon the acceptable sacrifice which Jesus was. We see throughout the Bible that God does in fact like and approve an appropriate sacrifice. We find this when Noah offered a sacrifice that was pleasing to God—the Scripture tells us that he built an altar and offered clean animals after leaving the ark after the days of the flood. This sacrifice was so pleasing that the Lord smelled it, receiving it with pleasure.

In the same way as Noah, Jesus giving His life as the sin offering was pleasing to God and the appropriate sacrifice which gave Abba no reason to look away. This is also true of our lives when we give them to the Lord as a pleasing sacrifice in righteousness. They become a pure, pleasing aroma that blesses the Lord's heart and will bless our lives as a result! This helps us understand why the sacrificial lamb was offered each year for the sins of Israel, and why Jesus was the appropriate sacrifice as the perfect Lamb of God. God didn't look away from the lamb offered nor did He look away from His Son, Jesus.

Jesus was the pleasing sacrifice of God, being received by Him and not giving Him a reason to look away. So just who then turned away the day Jesus was crucified? Was it Abba or man? Isaiah 53 gives another prophetic account of Jesus the Messiah and the horrible things He would suffer when He agreed to die for all. It also reveals that it was man who rejected Him and turned away. There is no mention at all of God turning away: *"He is despised and rejected of men; a man of sorrows, and acquainted with grief: and **we hid as it were our faces from Him**; He was despised, and we esteemed Him not"* (Isa. 53:3).

Sadly, this is still true today! It is man who turns away from God, but it is God who keeps pursuing us in the midst of our sin and suffering.

When Abba Hides His Face

What does it mean for God to hide His face or to show His face? When God shows His face, it means that He is proud, pleased, shows favor, approval, and blessings! However, to hide His face means an expression of alienation, being forsaken, rejected, cursed, shown wrath, anger, judgment, and a turning away because of our sins. God hides His face from individuals in disapproval of their sin and lifestyle, causing the dynamics of their relationship to change until they seek to do what was right in His eyes.

The "turning one's face away" in the Bible was the removing of one's presence from a person. In Hebrew, the words translated *face* and *presence* are the same word, *panim*. The hiding of His face in Hebrew is *hester panim*. In Psalm 51, when David sinned and repented, he said, "Do not remove or take away Your Spirit from me" (see Ps. 51:11). This is the same idea or sense of the term we are referring to concerning the idea of Abba turning His face away from Jesus. He didn't turn His face away from His Son because Jesus always did what pleased His Father, including His death on the cross. So there was no need for Abba to look away!

When determining if Abba hid His face from Jesus, it helps to know how this concept came about in the first place. The hiding of the face appears initially when Adam and Eve hid themselves from God's presence. It was initiated by *their* sinful actions, not God's! They were the ones who hid from the face of God after eating from the tree of knowledge of good and evil (see Gen. 3: 8).

Another example is the punishment following Cain's murder of his brother, Abel. God asks Cain, *"Why is your face downcast?"* (Gen. 4:6 NIV). It is Cain who needs to adjust his heart and face; it was not the Lord that was turning His face away from him. We see this when Cain finally admits his guilt of killing his brother and is the one suggesting that God will now turn His face from him: *"Behold, Thou hast driven me out this day from the face of the earth; and from Thy face shall I be hid"* (Gen. 4:14). The mere mention of the hiding of the face of God represented a lack of blessings, disapproval, and disappointment between God and Cain.

God hid His face from His people when there was ongoing sin, saying that He would hide His face because of all the evils they had done and turning to other gods (see Deut. 31:18). But He would forgive them if they would turn to Him, change, and repent.

We live in such a sinful world and it is growing darker each and every day. This is why we must stay close to Abba with a continued relentless pursuit of Him. It is far better to live our lives in purity than in sin. Sin affects our outlook on life and our relationship with God—this is why some feel forsaken, ashamed, and have discontinued walking with the Lord. When people choose to live a life in sin, some will often feel like the tax collector that Jesus spoke about in the parable—feeling so ashamed of themselves, their sins, and lifestyle. They don't feel worthy to call upon God or even consider Him, so why even try? In this story, Jesus tells us that the tax collector wouldn't even look up to Heaven because he was a sinner: *"But the tax collector stood at a distance. He would not even look up to heaven, but beat his breast and said, 'God, have mercy on me, a sinner'"* (Luke 18:13 NIV).

Doesn't this describe the approach many have concerning Abba in our day? They can't look to Heaven because they question whether or not He will even hear them. So they cry out, hoping for God's mercy to help them. Yet, we don't have to feel or live this way! When we are saved through Jesus Christ and His forgiveness, we are already seated with Him in heavenly places (see Eph. 2:6). This means we don't have to look up to Heaven as someone unworthy like the tax collector did. We are already spiritually seated with Jesus and declared worthy and righteous because of His shed blood that has given grace and mercy to all who will receive it.

Abba loves us and considers us as one of His own children! So we don't ever have to hold our head down low or look up to

Heaven hoping He hears us! No! We can come boldly to our heavenly Father's throne of grace and find grace and mercy to help in the time of need, no matter how many times we blow it! We can have confidence that He is there to help us through our struggles and the things we are facing!

So what happens when God hides His face in Scripture? Do you remember the story of the golden calf Aaron made while Moses was spending time in God's presence (see Exod. 32)? The people of Israel thought something had happened to Moses so they convinced Aaron to make a golden calf. This, of course, made the Lord very angry as well as Moses. The Lord told Moses to go down from the mountain where he was fellowshipping with Him and see how the people had corrupted themselves. After seeing the false god they made and their sinful behavior, Moses, in his anger, threw the commandments that the Lord wrote with His finger to the ground, breaking them. This didn't make God very happy because He made Moses rewrite them by hand the second time!

Aaron, knowing that he was guilty of listening to the people and creating this golden calf, began to make an excuse that is quite amusing. He told his brother that he threw all the gold he had received from the people into the fire, and out came this calf. Yeah, right. Anyway, God was angry with the people and it took Moses's intercession to keep Him from wiping them all out. What God did was turn His back upon them until they were willing to change and obey Him.

Do you remember when Moses wanted to see God's glory in the next chapter (see Exod. 33:18)? God responded by telling him that he couldn't see His face, but rather His back. Why? Perhaps it was to show Moses all the events of creation so he could write the first five books of the Old Testament with an eyewitness account, if you will. Or perhaps it was because God was saying, "I have turned My back upon Israel and the only way for you and them to see My face is to follow Me. I am turning and showing you My back as their leader. This is to see if they will follow Me and follow you. It is to see if they will listen to Me and desire to be with Me."

This is what it means when God turns His back throughout Scripture. It is not for the purpose of abandonment, but rather to see if the people will return to Him and follow Him on His terms, not theirs.

Let's consider the example we mentioned with Moses and God and how it relates to God turning His face away. One of the first things that happens when He turns His face away is that the dynamic of the relationship and His blessings change! What do I mean by this? Think for a moment: if God only allows Moses to see His back as He said, then this would mean that if they are facing each other face to face, then God would have to turn His back. Watch how the relationship changes and what is now affected by this action. Again, visualize God walking past Moses looking forward and Moses being behind Him. Moses is then seeing God's back from behind Him. Notice the placement of the very things we need in our intimate pursuit of God and our relationship with Him. Where are God's hands, mouth, eyes, ears, and feet? What direction are they facing? They are all facing forward as God is showing Moses His back and not His face.

This action was to show God's displeasure of Israel's rebellious, purposeful, sinful conduct in creating and worshipping the false god of the golden calf. This is the very reason God will show His back or turn His face away from His people. It was to get people to examine their hearts and their paths, just as it was with Israel. If we want His eyes to see us, His ears to hear us,

His hands to bless us, His mouth to speak to us, and His feet to guide us, then we need to change our hearts and follow Him.

The reason He turned His face away with Moses and Israel was to get them to decide if they wanted the benefits of these things in their relationship with Him or not. And it is the same for us today. When God turns His face and shows His back, it changes the way He speaks and how we hear Him; it changes His blessings and how we receive them; and it will change how He looks upon our life as one that is pleasing or displeasing before Him.

So, then, how does one see His face and not His back? They must turn and follow Him by changing their hearts. God turned His face in the Bible to get them to change their heart, direction, and follow Him so He could bless them. Again, just because God turned His face did not mean that they were forsaken or abandoned, but rather the dynamic of the relationship had changed.

You can still be with someone if you turn your back on them. The only thing that has changed is the dynamic of how you communicate, how you interact, and how you feel when this action is taking place. The intimacy changes because you no longer speak to their face but their back. This causes the dynamics of the relationship and blessings to change as well. God turns His face today, not in the sense of forsaking or abandonment, but rather in regards to His displeasure with sin.

Remember that in the New Testament God deals with sin through the blood of Jesus and His grace. So this doesn't mean God won't deal with sin or it is any less dangerous to us or displeasing to Him. What it means is that He will point us in a new direction so we will follow Him and turn from the evil of our own ways. Additionally, it causes us to live our lives under the lordship of His Son and not according to our own ways.

Today, if God should turn His face so His back is revealed to us, it is to remind us of the bloodied back of the Son of God that took our sins, shame, curse, and sickness upon Himself. It is to remind us of the grace available through His blood and that we have victory over a life of sin. It is to show us that we have a choice to walk righteously and intimately with Him. Or we can choose not to as well. It also forces those who want His blessings to turn to Him and follow Him on His terms and not their own.

This causes us to be more determined to be blessed by Him because, if His back is what we are seeing, then it means His hands are facing forward, turned away from us. So if you want His blessings, you must change and pursue Him. What a rewarding life when you follow Him to seek His face and please Him. It's not works of righteousness but loving, honorable, righteous living from our hearts! When you do that, He will turn and bless you! Yet, we don't want to cause Him, like He did with Moses, to show us His back because our lives aren't pleasing to Him. If He does, it is to get us to adjust our lives because we are in sin and disobedience against Him. As long as we keep seeking His face, we don't have to be concerned with seeing His back.

Let's look at what happens when Abba shows His face:

1. You see His eyes (His approval, affirmation, and protection):

   Keep me as the apple of Your eye; hide me in the shadow of Thy wings (Psalm 17:8).

   I will instruct thee and teach thee in the way which thou shalt go: I will guide thee with Mine eye (Psalm 32:8).

   The eyes of the Lord are upon the righteous, and His ears are open unto their cry (Psalm 34:15).

2. He gives you His ears (your prayers are answered):

   The eyes of the Lord are upon the righteous, and His ears are open unto their cry (Psalm 34:15).

3. He opens His mouth to speak and bless you (you hear His voice and love).

4. His nostrils smell a pleasing aroma (His pleasure, delight, approval, and He gives you a fresh start):

   And the Lord smelled a sweet savour; and the Lord said in His heart, I will not again curse the ground any more for man's sake... (Genesis 8:21).

5. His hands will be open to bless you (His touch, His presence, His healing, and His blessings upon your life).

6. His feet accompany you (His intervention, His authority over your enemies and problems, He will walk before you, giving direction, wisdom, and guidance).

I want you to be encouraged and press into Abba's face, His love, and acceptance of you! I want you to hunger for His face more and more and not live in fear that He will hide His face from you. The Lord blesses the righteous and His ears are open to their cry! So remember that there is no longer a separation between God and mankind. You don't need to try to earn His love or approval. It's already yours through Jesus! Abba longs to reveal His heart and His love to you. He wants you to see Him, feel His presence, and hear the tenderness of His whisper that speaks to you!

Abba didn't turn away from His Son and He won't turn His face away as we seek Him and commit to living a life pleasing to Him. Seek Him and you will find Him; ask and you will receive of His blessings; and knock on the doors of His throne room and they will be opened to you in abundance (see Matt. 7:7). His heart is for you to love and search deeper in order to know Him. His face is for you to enjoy so you can discover a more intimate relationship with Him as your heavenly Daddy! He is reaching out, wanting to show Himself strong on your behalf. His heart is calling out to you. So go ahead let your heart continue to cry out to Him again and again, saying, "Abba, my heart cries for *You!*"

Chapter Eight

Daddy First!

*Jesus saith unto her, Touch Me not; for I am
not yet ascended to My Father: but go to My
brethren, and say unto them, I ascend unto
My Father, and your Father; and to My God,
and your God* (John 20:17).

It is finished! Now let the angels sing, the earth rejoice, and let the people return unto their heavenly Father! This is because what Abba had planned through His Son was coming to an end—it would be complete!

After declaring that it is finished, Jesus lifts Himself up to speak His last few words upon the cross. His eyes are blackened, swollen shut from the beatings He took from the hands of men. Blood has now dried upon His brow, making it difficult to see. He squints, and with determination opens His eyes as wide as He can to gaze up into the heavens. He knows His Father is with Him and focuses with great intensity as if to look deep into Abba's eyes. *This is the reason I have been spared, the reason I have been kept,* He would rehearse in His heart.

Now with great focus and His heart full of complete trust and love for His heavenly Daddy, He would open His eyes and His mouth to speak.

His lips cut, bruised, bloodied, and swollen didn't stop Him from speaking His final words to His Abba from the cross. He cries out to His heavenly Daddy who has been waiting for this very moment. Jesus speaks loudly for all to hear—in Heaven, on the earth, and in hell. He calls out to Abba, *"Father, into Thy hands I commend My spirit"* (Luke 23:46). It would be with these words that He would breathe His last breath upon the cross.

Those words echo throughout that which is visible and invisible, piercing through darkness and sending forth light. The earth begins to shake at this very announcement from His lips. The devil and his evil hordes are alarmed at these words as they are reverberating throughout Heaven, hell, and the earth.

At the very moment Jesus speaks these final words, the veil in the temple is torn in two, from the top to bottom. It causes the earth to shake as its foundations are moved! The tombs are opened as those who have died are raised from the dead as a witness testifying of the risen Savior (see Matt. 27:52)! And those by the cross are unable to stand, shaking in fear, trembling and terrified! A Roman centurion, visibly shaken by the events taking place, gazes upon Jesus's lifeless body that is still hanging on the cross. He declares with awe, *"Truly this man was the Son of God"* (Mark 15:39).

What is happening? Why is there such chaos in hell and the earth, but yet such celebration in Heaven? Something so powerful has just taken place. At that very moment the spiritual veil that separated God and man was torn in two. The very reflection of this spiritual veil is now taking place in the earth as the veil of the temple is also ripped in half! Why the tearing of these veils, both in Heaven and on earth? It is because there is no longer separation between God and man. Such jubilation, celebration, and rejoicing as Jesus offered His life and would now be raised from the dead. Abba is showing His face reaching for His lost creation as the veil is removed! It was not just His announcement that tore these veils, but it was also Jesus's heart crying for Abba on our behalf! It took place so that all mankind could discover their heavenly Daddy in a more personal way! Now our hearts can cry, "Abba, Father!"

When this veil was torn, it was Jesus committing all things to His Father, and Abba reaching back to His lost creation through the blood of Jesus. The natural veil in the temple was torn into two from top to bottom because it was showing Abba was initiating the tearing, expressing His desire to be with mankind. It was revealing that He was reaching toward the human race and that is why it was torn in this fashion. It was also to show that Abba, who sits upon His throne in Heaven, longed to be reconciled to His creation again!

God the Father was so excited to have His sons and daughters now reconciled with Him that He received the very sin sacrifice of His Son's redeeming blood that day on the cross. Once Jesus said it is finished, that it is accomplished, and committed His spirit into His Father's hand, it immediately caused the veil in the temple to be torn! Again, it is our Abba, our Daddy, our heavenly Father reaching down for us! We can run into His arms, seek His face, and climb in His lap to receive His love! It is because this veil is torn that there is no longer a separation of sin that keeps us from our heavenly Daddy. We no longer need to go through an earthly priesthood or need the blood sacrifice of an animal to give us access to God. This is because Jesus made the way, and He became the only way to Abba by becoming sin's sacrifice and being the Lamb of God who takes away all the sins of mankind!

The mere fact that this veil was torn from the top to bottom and not bottom to top shows God was the one reaching toward us who are in the earth. It was as if His arms were reaching from Heaven to bring us to the place of His loving arms and revealing His face in the throne room. It gives us the awesome privilege to come boldly now to His throne of grace, and receive grace, help, and mercy from our heavenly Daddy in times of need! When understanding what took place with the tearing of this veil, it is important to understand just how impossible it was for it to be torn in this fashion. It was not an act of man, but rather a supernatural act of Abba!

You see, scholars, especially the renowned historian Josephus, say that the veil was about 60 feet high, 20 feet wide, with the thickness of about four inches and weighing about four tons. He documents that the veil was renewed every year, and that horses tied to each side could not pull it apart. It took 300 men just to hold it. God had this veil designed like this on purpose; to show that only He could tear it apart and what His loving intent toward us was in doing so.

This is why it would be impossible for man to tear it. But what is more interesting is that at the precise instant the veil was torn, some historians believe, was at the exact moment the priests were in the temple preparing the evening sacrifice. Can you imagine the look on their faces as this veil is torn in half and God accepts the evening sacrifice of His Son, Jesus Christ, for the sins of mankind forever, once and for all!

This is why we are called sons and daughters through faith in Jesus Christ (see Gal. 3:26). It is because the spiritual and natural veils are no more! There is nothing that can separate us from the love of our Abba. We have full and complete access to Him!

Daddy First

Praise God that this veil is torn and Jesus is alive! God has fulfilled His word to man and His plan to redeem them is also fulfilled. Abba has been with Jesus throughout His life and through the events of the crucifixion, showing once again that He would not leave His side. He would be with Him as His body would not suffer any decay or be left in hell, and He would be raised from the dead! The psalmist declared:

> *I have set the Lord always before me: because He is at my right hand, I shall not be moved. Therefore my heart is glad, and my glory rejoiceth: my flesh also shall rest in hope. For Thou wilt not leave my soul in hell; neither wilt Thou suffer Thine Holy One to see corruption* (Psalm 16:8-10).

Something so significant and special that reveals Jesus's love and the heart of Abba is about to take place. What would it be?

There is a sound of despair coming from an empty tomb that once contained the body of Jesus. He is not dead, but very much alive by the power of God's hand. Yet, Mary Magdalene, the former prostitute and friend of Jesus who was gloriously delivered from the hand of the enemy (see Mark 16:9), is now weeping and sobbing. She is shaken, upset, and feeling as though her Lord has been torn from her life. She approaches the empty tomb with a sense of hopelessness and despair. Doesn't she remember the words that Jesus said that He is the resurrection and the life, and those who believe in Him though they die will live with Him for eternity?

She is trembling and wiping tears from her eyes. She bends down to look into the empty tomb and sees two angels dressed in white, seated where Jesus's body had been—one at the head and the other at the foot. "Woman, why are you weeping?" asks one of the angels. Mary Magdalene, about to burst into tears, replies, "They have taken my Lord away, and I don't know where they have put Him."

She then hears another voice speaking to her, but thinking it is the gardener turns to this strangely familiar sound, not realizing it is Jesus. He says to her, "Woman, why are you crying? Who are you looking for?" She is not in the frame of mind or mood to answer questions but desperately wants to know where Jesus's body is. So she asks, "Sir, if you have carried Him away, tell me where you have put Him, and I will get Him." Jesus can hardly hold back His smile and His heart of love for her as He responds, "Mary, it is I!" Mary is so overcome with joy, surprise, and jubilation that she wants nothing more than to hug and hold her Lord.

However, Jesus responds to her with something so powerful and so amazing for you and me. It is the heart of Abba revealed and will surely cause our hearts to cry out to Him! Jesus responds to her, "Mary, do not hold onto Me, for I have not yet ascended to the Father." He then sends her to tell the rest of the disciples and others that He is alive; but before He does, I want you to notice the awesome words He tells her: "I am ascending to My Father and your Father, to My God and your God" (see John 20:17)!

Do you see those amazing words? "My Father, your Father; My God, your God"? Doesn't it make your heart cry out for Him? Notice how Jesus reveals Abba first! He doesn't say, "My God, your God" first, but rather, "My Father, your Father!" He is saying, "Abba will not only be your almighty, powerful God, but He is Daddy first! He will be there for you, to love you, care for you, and spend time with in you every waking day! He is your heavenly Daddy and He is committed to a more personal and intimate life with you!"

I tell you that this is too good to pass up! What amazing love, friendship, kindness, and care to know He is our heavenly Daddy first. This is important in our relationship with Him and is why Jesus is revealing this in the way He phrased His words to Mary. He wanted her and everyone to know Abba is our heavenly Daddy, and when we accept Him, all the great attributes of Him as our God are available for our benefit. This is why Jesus told us not to fear as His little flock because, after all, it is our Abba's good pleasure to give us the Kingdom (see Luke 12:32)!

What Jesus spoke to Mary Magdalene is so personal, intimate, and profound. Jesus is revealing Abba's heart so we can know Him as our personal Daddy before we understand Him as the all-powerful and majestic One.

Remember the first two questions Abba asked Adam and Eve in the Garden? It was God declaring His desire for relationship, first by asking Adam where he was after he sinned, and then it was followed by the provision of the animal coats to cover them, after asking them who it was that told them they were naked. These questions again were to reveal God in a personal relationship, followed by His benefits and provision.

We see the same thing when Jesus came to Mary Magdalene. He appeared to her before anyone else, mentioning, "My Abba, your Abba" first to show the importance of an intimate, personal relationship with Him, followed by an understanding that He is God. It is interesting that He appeared to her first. Have you ever thought why He appeared to her before anyone else? Why was it that a former prostitute saw Him first, rather than someone considered more prominent like the rich man, Joseph of Arimathea, who rented his tomb for the use of Jesus's burial or even someone else? We know that God is no respecter of persons, but it does show us something special about His heart and love. By choosing a former prostitute, perhaps Jesus wanted to reveal Abba to those who feel as though they have done things so shameful and so bad that they think God doesn't love them or accept them. Maybe it was to give hope to mankind that Abba forgives and desires to restore people whose lives have been broken.

This is why He spoke those precious words to Mary after He arose from the dead, saying, "Don't touch me yet, Mary, for I haven't yet ascended to *My* Daddy and your Daddy, *My* God and your God." He is showing His Daddy's love for us and how much He wants us to love Him, know Him, and cherish Him more than the benefits He gives to us. Religion has taught us wrongly, and oftentimes even backward. It often teaches us that God is an all-powerful being who is impatient, so powerful, and unapproachable. Some say He is a Father but not with a revelation of Abba, our heavenly Papa!

Powerful Truths

There are some powerful truths we can learn from this first encounter of Jesus with Mary Magdalene and when He later appeared to the disciples in John 20. When He appeared to Mary Magdalene as she was alone at the tomb, it was significant in that it represents our individual understanding of the Lord and our personal relationship with God first and foremost (see John 20:1-18). It shows us the importance of knowing God as our Abba and not being afraid to refer to Him as such.

Jesus then appears in this same chapter to the disciples who are afraid, sitting in a room with the door locked. Some of them would become leaders in what would later become the first church. Even though the door is locked and the disciples are fearful, Jesus walks into the middle of the room supernaturally! The relevance for our day can be seen in that the church and leadership today must not lock out the Lord's presence like they did with the locking of the doors with the disciples. We must never close our hearts or churches from His supernatural power and presence. We should always make a place and room for Him to show up when He wants and how He wants. The key is that we need God's manifested supernatural presence and power in our churches and lives.

We can gain further insight from John 20 in what the Lord revealed to His disciples when He walked in among them. He told them to go and show others that He is alive and tell them what He has done: *"Then said Jesus to them again, Peace be unto you: as My Father hath sent Me, even so send I you"* (John 20:21). In other words, we need to let Him show up by telling others about Him and allowing Him to display His power though us. This is why Jesus spent time with His disciples after His resurrection—so they would go evangelize and reveal Him and Abba to the whole world, displaying His supernatural glory! John writes,

> *And many other signs truly did Jesus in the presence of His disciples, which are not written in this book: but these are written, that ye might believe that Jesus is the Christ, the Son of God; and that believing ye might have life through His name* (John 20:30-31).

No matter what setting, whether it be our own personal walk, in our churches, or in the lives of others, we must always remember that Jesus wants to be the Lord of our lives and He desires to reveal Abba in a more personal way. This is why we can cry, "Abba, Father" and tell others of His love!

The Cry for Abba

There is something so special, so pure, and so intimate about declaring to God that He is our Abba. When we do, it is like a magnet that pulls His Fatherly love to us. It changes the dynamic of our relationship with Him in a much more personal way. The cry from Jesus's heart to His heavenly Daddy can also be our cry today as well! Think about that for a moment? We can cry out from our heart to Him, saying, "Abba!" He longs to hear us speak that from our lips and He waits to hear it from mankind!

In fact, the moment we give our life to Jesus we have immediate access to our heavenly Father and His wonderful throne room. Something still more powerful takes place as well. There is a sound released out of our hearts to God that reconciles us back to Him. This is what the Scripture tells us takes place and why the Spirit cries out of us, "Abba, Father": *"And because ye are sons, God hath sent forth the Spirit of His Son into your hearts, crying, Abba, Father"* (Gal. 4:6).

This means we receive immediate sonship status with Him, causing a special intimacy with Him as our heavenly Daddy that is for the believer only! What does it mean that the Spirit cries within us, "Abba Father"? It means reconciliation between you and your heavenly Father takes place the moment you accept Jesus.

When looking at this verse in Galatians 4, we come to understand how powerful it is when the Spirit of God cries "Abba" through us. It also shows us that we can now, because of His Spirit, let our heart cry "Abba." It is not just a onetime event for the Holy Spirit to cry out in us at the time of our spiritual conversion to the Lord; nor is it to be a one time event or something we seldom do! We need to let our hearts cry out daily saying, "Abba!" We need not feel ashamed, embarrassed, or uncomfortable in prayer and fellowship with Him to call Him Abba. When we do, we come to realize the personal revelation of Him as our heavenly Daddy takes us to a greater level of intimacy with Him. We feel more secure, loved, affirmed, special, and close to Him as a result!

Notice that the word *cry* from this verse in Galatians 4 is *krázō* in the Greek, which is a term for a raven's piercing cry ("caw").[1] It is defined as "to cry out loudly with an urgent scream or shriek," by using "inarticulate shouts that express *deep* emotion."[2] How does this apply to us? The moment we give over our lives to Jesus, the Holy Spirit inside our spirit cries out, like with a loud scream, saying, "Abba, Father!" This means the first thing declared to our spirit and heard by our spiritual ears is the cry for our heavenly Daddy, Abba!

In other words, the Spirit of God does this through us when we are saved! Something so amazing happens in the heart of God that He expresses it by the cry of the Spirit in us. He is showing us by this cry of the Spirit that He so wants to be with us. He longs for all men to call upon His Son, who is the doorway to Him as our heavenly Daddy. God is so excited to be reconciled with His lost creation of mankind that His Spirit expresses this by screaming out loudly, "Abba!" It is such a tender, special moment for the Lord and for us.

This cry then becomes one of the strong foundations in which we as believers build our Christian life upon; it is the revelation of the heavenly Father. This is important in the life of a young believer just as much as the first thing a child learns to recognize and listen for is the voice of his or her parent. In the same way, this cry in our hearts enables us to call out to Abba, having the confidence and trust that He will hear us and provide for our needs. It is from this cry at the moment of our spiritual conversion that reveals our heavenly Daddy to us.

Something so powerful happens within us as we begin to hear His voice and sense His leading and presence. We become aware of His affirmation, love, and devotion to us. This is why it is important as a Christian to continue to let our heart cry, "Abba." When we do, we begin to understand our rights as His beloved spiritual children and how amazing He is as our Father. We begin to do what Jesus did when He walked the earth. We want our lives to emulate Him and will diligently seek to please Him more and more, causing Him to smile upon us with approval. We can do this because we are no longer strangers to Him but His dear children. He becomes a heavenly

Daddy to us and we become His spiritual sons and daughters (see 2 Cor. 6:18)!

As His children, through the new birth in Jesus Christ, we have rights and privileges that don't belong to those who are not of His royal family. For example, notice what we inherit and the process that takes place as we allow the cry of Abba to come from our hearts, especially at the time we ask Jesus to come into our hearts and lives and be Lord of all!

Now, because we are reconciled back to Abba through Jesus Christ, we become not only His children but Kingdom citizens with special rights and privileges in that Kingdom! For example:

- We can now call Him "Abba," our Father and heavenly Daddy: *"And because ye are sons, God hath sent forth the Spirit of His Son into your hearts, crying, Abba, Father"* (Gal. 4:6).

- We are spiritually adopted as His children and become spiritually born of God: *"For ye received not the spirit of bondage again unto fear; but ye received the Spirit of adoption, whereby we cry, Abba, Father"* (Rom. 8:15).

- We have a spiritual inheritance as His children and are joint-heirs with Jesus: *"And if children, then heirs; heirs of God, and joint-heirs with Christ; if so be that we suffer with Him, that we may be also glorified together"* (Rom. 8:17).

- We live in a household as His spiritual children and are under His care and provision: *"Now therefore ye are no more strangers and foreigners, but ye are fellow-citizens with the saints, and of the household of God"* (Eph. 2:19).

- We have a future home that awaits us as His beloved children: *"In My Father's house are many mansions; if it were not so, I would have told you; for I go to prepare a place for you"* (John 14:2).

Our hearts must continue to cry "Abba" day and night, in the good times and the challenging times! We can call Him Abba because we are His children and enjoy His benefits freely given to us. Never forget or underestimate the fact that you are His child when committing your life to His Son—that is what enables you to become His spiritual children. Again, this happened when Jesus died and rose from the dead, restoring the sonship that was lost with Adam! This was God's plan fulfilled and the promise given to Abraham and his children. All that was lost in Adam now becomes ours as His spiritual children in Christ. Adam was a son of God, and so are we sons and daughters of God when we accept His only begotten Son, Jesus.

How do we know this? Well, notice the genealogy of Jesus from the time of His birth dating back to the first man, Adam. In the last verse of the chapter it gives the names of the fathers and their sons. Yet, when you read Adam's name at the bottom, he is called the son of God. In other words, we can see from this example that Adam's Father is God and not a natural man. Adam, as a son of God, is born of God's Spirit:

> *The son of Cainan, the son of Arphaxed, the son of Shem, the son of Noah, the son of Lamech, the son of Methuselah, the son of Enoch, the son of Jared, the son of Mahalalel, the son of Kenan, the son of Enosh, the son of Seth, the son of Adam, the son of God* (Luke 3:36-38 NIV).

He was born of God when the Lord breathed His Spirit into him as a lifeless clay figure. It is the same way for us today. Even though we are conceived from a natural biological father, we can become spiritually born again from our heavenly Father.

Just like Adam, who was born of God's Spirit, so are we. *"Jesus answered, Verily, verily, I say unto thee, Except a man be born of water and of the Spirit, he cannot enter into the kingdom of God"* (John 3:5).

When we are saved and born again, God breathes His Spirit into us, causing us to cry out "Abba," and reconnecting us with our heavenly Abba! We become a spiritual son or daughter of God! This is why Adam is called the "son" of God! In the same way as others in the earth may be a son of their natural father, but when they are born again they become a spiritually reborn son of Abba! This is why the Scripture tells us, *"How great is the love the Father has lavished on us, that we should be called children of God! And that is what we are! The reason the world does not know us is that it did not know Him"* (1 John 3:1 NIV).

Our hearts cry "Abba" because we know Him and He knows us; we are His children and He is our Father! Once we understand that, there is no limit to His love in our lives and our knowledge of who He is. The key is that we must continue to let our hearts cry out to Him, "Abba, Father!"

Spending Time With Abba

Now that we have come to know Him and see Him revealed as our Abba, our personal heavenly Daddy, we want to run to Him and be safe! We lean upon Him as our pillar of strength. We come to Him to comfort us in times of trouble; and we fellowship with Him with a deep hunger that searches for the innermost parts of His heart that few have come to discover.

This is because He is our Abba, and He is like no other! His arms are open to receive us at any moment and any time. He waits for us to shut the door to the busyness of our lives and talk with Him, sing to Him, share our hearts with Him in secret. He waits every day to see what we will say the moment we open our eyes. Will we say, "Abba"? Let's spend time with Him and enjoy the lasting benefits of knowing Him as our heavenly Daddy in a more personal way!

Never forget that He is our Daddy first! Sure, He is almighty God, our Father. But He is first your heavenly Daddy and is committed to stay at your side and be ever-present in your times of need. He so wants you to know Him as your personal Abba more intimately! He is your heavenly Papa and Father!

All through creation and throughout Scripture His heart has been for you to see Abba revealed. There is no longer any separation or barrier to keep us from Him unless we let it. Doesn't your heart cry out for Him today? It is this cry that is the greatest longing from the heart of those who are hungry to truly understand Him and know Him as their heavenly Daddy. Once we cry out with every ounce of breath we have, we can now love Him, approach Him, and spend time with Him on an ever-increasing basis! His eye is upon you and His ear is open to your heart. He's waiting for your heart to cry out to Him, "Abba!"

Let's go for it, let's start now! "Abba, my heart cries for *You!*"

Notes

1. This definition is taken from *Strong's Concordance,* #2896.

2. *WS,* 708.